NEWBRIDGE

LECHLADE

OXFORD

CRICKLADE

ABINGDON

SHILLINGFORD

The River Thames

PANGBOURNE

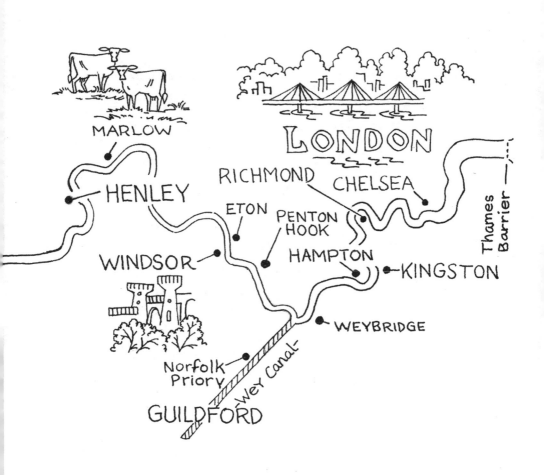

MARLOW

LONDON

HENLEY

RICHMOND CHELSEA

ETON

PENTON
HOOK

WINDSOR

HAMPTON

KINGSTON

Thames
Barrier

WEYBRIDGE

Norfolk
Priory

Wey Canal

GUILDFORD

DISCOVERING ENGLAND

Discovering England

from One Inch above the Thames

Jim Payne

Lytton Publishing Company

Contents

Preface

My first connection with England came through Gilbert and Sullivan. At the age of 4, I listened for hours to songs from their operettas, playing 78 rpm records on an old electric Victrola. I could never seem to get enough of their bouncy rhythms and zany lyrics, and wound up memorizing for life many of their most famous numbers. Even at that tender age, I marveled at their irreverent, ironic tone. A modern major general who knows as much about gunnery as a novice in a nunnery! An office boy who polished the handle of the big front door so carefully that now he is the ruler of the Queen's navy!

Today, aware of the stuffy 19th-century era in which they wrote, I am even more amazed at their impudence. Remember, they were spoofing generals and admirals in the heyday of the British Empire. In another country, Gilbert and Sullivan would have been put in jail, or at least shunned for making light of the majesty of the state and its officials. But not in England. The operettas were immensely popular, and the generals and admirals laughed along with everyone else.

How did such a funny country come into being, a nation that considers laughing at itself a protected national pastime? The answer, I think, lies in the multitude of inconsistencies that abound. When nations were made, God sprinkled the available traits and virtues here and there. When it came to England, He changed His approach and scattered tiny seeds of contradiction that settled deeply into the soil. At first nothing seemed amiss. The Saxons didn't notice anything, and I don't think the Romans did either. But after a time, these inconsistencies began to sprout, here and there, like dandelions in the lawn, more and more, until there was nothing anyone could do about them. Thus did the English surrender to irony.

Here's a tiny example of what I'm talking about. In London's Trafalgar Square stands a proud statue of Charles I. At the other end of the street connecting the square to the Houses of Parliament is a proud statue of Oliver Cromwell, the man who executed Charles I. People of logical lands would exclaim, "Hey, wait a minute. They both can't be considered right and venerated!" The English, long ago overwhelmed by the dandelions, merely smile. One wit, his tongue deeply in his cheek, said the contradiction was "an example of our attempts to be fair to everybody."

Many writers have traveled across England trying to get to the bottom of this awkwardly original country, using many means of locomotion. They have walked across its length, and walked across its breadth. They have taken branch railways to the end of the line. And of course they have toured by cars—when they could find a place to park. Through all these methods, a great deal of progress has been made unraveling England's mysteries.

Yet there is another means of transportation to be explored, a device so alien as to be a kind of English joke itself: the kayak, a wood and canvas contraption invented by the Aleutian Indians. In this vessel, we can literally get to the bottom of England, suspending ourselves at water level, to direct our gaze upward at monuments, people, and culture. Perhaps in this slender, silent craft we shall be able to sneak up on some new discoveries in this most delightfully puzzling land.

Let's see what happens.

I

In Love with Quaint

The swan came tearing at me, pedaling and splashing across the top of the water, flapping its wings. At first, I thought I had frightened it, and that it was trying to take off and flee. But no, the bird didn't want to be airborne. It wanted to frighten *me*, to make me think it was going to crash into me, and it nearly did, skidding to a splash landing right at the bow of my kayak. I could hardly believe it. Being attacked by a swan on the River Thames?! It seemed like a bizarre dream.

Before this encounter, I had always thought of swans as harmless, graceful, and nearly static decorations of ponds and lakes. And having seen them only from a distance, I had also thought of swans as rather small, about the size of ducks. Now I was suddenly discovering they were vigorous, fierce animals—and also surprisingly large. The swan charging at me with outstretched wings wasn't as big as a C-47 cargo plane, but that's the image that came to mind. This creature, I learned as I paddled a few yards farther, was angry because I was approaching the hen who was sitting upon their nest, a great throne of tightly woven straw placed atop driftwood at a narrow spot of the river. As I approached her, she became as angry as her mate, puffing up her feathers, hissing, and darting her sinuous neck from side to side like a cobra, seeking the right moment to hack me with her beak. I leaned far to the side away from her as my boat slid by.

I was just beginning my kayak trip down the Thames on the wildest part, in the stretch after Cricklade. The river here, close to the source, is so shallow that no powerboats can pass. The river was about eight feet wide where I put in, and for the first miles, overhanging trees blocked much of the sky.

Twice I had to get out of my kayak and drag it over the shallow, stony bottom. In another place, a log had fallen across the river, and I had to lift the boat over it. Steep banks of mud enclosed the river. Where the land was open, I saw only cows at pasture and an occasional barn. Apparently no one had found the Thames here sufficiently scenic to be worth building a house alongside it.

It seemed that in this relatively primitive environment, God's creatures were behaving as they would in a precivilized state. Every quarter mile or so, I came across a pair of swans who had staked out an exclusive territory. Most of these pairs were protecting already hatched cygnets, endearingly cute in their delicate gray fur. Farther down the river, this traditional family structure—mom, dad, and the kids in the log cabin out in the wilderness—disappeared. The swans became more sociable, gathering in groups as if adapting to the amenities of civilization. When I got to Lechlade, 18 miles downstream from Cricklade, where the river deepens and holiday makers abound, the first thing I saw was a dozen swans flocking toward the outstretched hand of a tourist feeding them bread crumbs.

Why am I paddling the River Thames, challenging its wildlife, and exploring its shores with my bottom balanced just one inch above its rippling waters?

The Thames holds for me the opportunity to delve into the mystery of England. It's been a lifelong pursuit of mine, this effort to pin down the quality that sets the English people apart. To me, the logical place to carry out this search for the soul of England is the Thames valley, the heart of England, where the river first tied together early settlements into the rudiments of a civilization.

My love affair with England began at the age of 17, and it was a case of love at first sight—or, to be strictly accurate, at first light. It was 1957, and I had come to England as an exchange student, brought by the English-Speaking Union to attend Highgate, a public school in north London (a "private" school in American-speak). We American students—about 20 of us, each headed for a different school—came over as a group on the Cunard liner *Queen Elizabeth* (the original one). The boat docked at Southampton late at night, so we could see nothing of the country from the windows of the boat train that took us to London. Fog and drizzle enshrouded the taxi I took from the station in London, so I remained surrounded by terra incognita on the trip to the hotel.

The next morning, I jumped out of bed, pulled back the drapes from the window, and looked out over the rooftops of the city. I practically screamed with delight. The English may take their roofs for granted, but to this American boy, they were unbelievably quaint, with their slate-covered gables, ornamented eaves and ridge lines, and, especially, chimney pots—stretching by the hundreds and thousands as far as the eye could see!

In the United States, there are none of these ornamented ceramic cylinders that grace the English skyline. American homes have plain old brick chimneys, with nothing decorating the tops of them. The only time Americans see chimney pots is in children's books that depict the gingerbread cottages where the Seven Dwarfs and Red Riding Hood lived. As I gazed out over those intricate, real-life rooftops, I felt I had been transported into the middle of a fairy tale.

This feeling about England never left me. It has something to do with the age of the place, with buildings that date back centuries, but it's more than that. I've seen stone structures in the Middle East much older than those England typically offers, yet the Middle Eastern monoliths leave me unmoved. I don't get a sense of the culture of the people who assembled them. In England, the oldish buildings in the streets and lanes project the values of the builders and the owners. They are quaint. Quirky. Whimsical. Independent.

This quality pervades many aspects of English life, not just the buildings. You see the quirkiness exhibited in the layout of towns and streets, in the plumbing—even in the hotel linen supply, and, if you can believe it, in English computers. Getting to the bottom of this mystery of why England often does things in quaint, original, and, yes, sometimes awkward ways was one of the objects of my journey.

In nautical terms, the distance from Cricklade to the Thames Barrier is 170 miles, a route that, if speed be desired, a kayak can cover in a week or less. It could be traveled even faster in other human-powered craft: a Thames skiff, for example. This very traditional—and still popular—wooden boat carries two rowers and two passengers who sit on a bench in the stern and control the tiller. Near Oxford, I met a rowing party in two skiffs who were aiming to accomplish the distance from Lechlade to Teddington, near London, in five days. They were young architects—four men and two women—who were carrying out a fundraiser for the Society of Antiquaries of London, an organization that works to preserve ancient buildings. By that point in my journey, I had become a fan of William Morris, a founder of the society a century ago, and a man these idealistic designers considered a patron saint. I was finding that his visionary ideas also spoke to me, and I surprised the rowers, who assumed I didn't know William Morris from Adam, by donating £20 to their cause.

Although most boaters may need to rush down the Thames to get back to their busy lives, my aim was to dawdle. I had set aside 29 days for the trip, and intended to pass extra time in towns and villages along the route to socialize and explore.

And though most travelers insist on knowing where they will rest their weary heads at night, I sought a journey with no commitments: no set times to arrive anywhere and no accommodations arranged. I planned to find a B&B when the time came, or to camp out using my plastic ground cloth and lightweight sleeping bag, or, if camping proved impossible, to huddle in the rain and mope.

I don't particularly enjoy not knowing where I'm going to sleep, nor do I look forward to an evening spent in rainy, muddy misery. But over the years, I've found traveling spontaneously thrusts me into contact with other human beings. I find that a scheduled trip, with hotels and transportation laid out beforehand, can be rather sterile. You don't need to talk to anyone, except perhaps to tell the waiter you want the bleu cheese dressing. In an unplanned trip, you must ask for advice and perhaps for help; in this way, you meet people, many of whom become guides, teachers, and friends.

Finally, this trip was, like all my kayak journeys, a solo enterprise. I do not have a dogmatic rule about this. I have on more than one occasion invited people to accompany me on a trip, but without success. Though this slightly injures my self-esteem, I have in the end come to the conclusion that the solo voyage is the most rewarding. It produces more challenges, more seemingly impossible fixes to get yourself out of. And because locals tend to take a special interest in a lone kayaker, one gets to meet more people.

To some degree, the interest of bystanders comes from compassion. On my trips, I am frequently taken for a homeless person, a judgment that can be rather embarrassing. Yet I must concede that in the essence of things, that judgment is substantially correct. On my journeys, I am indeed homeless, marked by the insecurity of not belonging anywhere—and dressing the part with my rather unkempt grooming and long-worn clothing. Furthermore, I am beyond the age of a student who might be expected to travel rough. When I am seen sleeping beside a footpath wrapped in a ground cloth, or struggling to carry my kayak pack—all my worldly possessions—on streets and trains, I see sympathy and embarrassment in the faces of passersby. On some occasions, I believe if I had set out an empty container, people would have dropped coins into it.

So the solo kayak journey, engrossing and exhilarating as it can be, is also a lesson in humility. Monks of old used to rend their garments and prostrate themselves on cold stone floors to gain perspective, and perhaps something of the same benefit accrues to me, promoting a mood of confident resignation. When the world has taken you for a beggar, you know there's not much more you can do to disappoint it.

2
Common Courtesy

In the early days of the trip, I worried a great deal about the response I might provoke by my practice of commando camping, which is the name kayakers give to the practice of spending the night on private land without permission. If detected, would I be assaulted by angry farmers waving pitchforks? Would packs of hounds be unleashed to devour me? I didn't have any read on how uptight the English might be about their private property rights—especially when these rights were being infringed by an American.

On my first night on the river I camped out, but I made no contact with the natives. I was paddling the stretch just below Cricklade, where the countryside is lightly populated, and chose a campsite location densely screened by trees and entirely hidden from buildings and roads. This piece of English forest bore the marks of civilization, however. Stock grazing had cleared away the underbrush, and someone had run a mower through the grass to create a bridleway—which gave me a clear space to spread my ground cloth. I also could hear recorded music coming from an open window of a distant house, as well as car traffic on a road a quarter mile away. But I saw no one, and I'm pretty sure no one saw me.

One notable feature of this relatively rural campsite was the profusion of birdsong. In the evening and on the following morning, the forest exploded with tweeting and warbling from all around. Knowing nothing about the particular birds behind these calls, or their habits, I felt mystified. To my ear, it was like overhearing conversations in a Chinese marketplace, with many buyers and sellers engaged in intricate haggling over unknown wares. This abundance of birdsong, incidentally, exceeded anything I can recall hearing in the United States, either in the East or West. For example, on hikes in my home forests in Idaho, even in the spring when birds are especially vocal, I typically hear only occasional birdcalls, usually in the distance.

Another contrast concerned mosquitoes: There were hardly any! In damp areas in the United States, these pesky insects abound, especially in the spring. I had brought along a vial of insect repellent, expecting a similar challenge here. But I never had to use it. At first, I thought these pests were extinct in the land, killed off by glaciers of old or extinguished by some patron saint who wanted to give Britons a special break. But this wasn't the case, for I occasionally saw one. Perhaps the explanation for their rarity is that England's great multitudes of songbirds gobble almost all of them up.

A peaceful, undisturbed camping setup such as I had that first night was a rare find, for it required a number of favorable conditions: some distance from people, roads, footpaths, houses, livestock, and dogs; visual protection from the world's prying eyes in the form of trees and shrubs; and ground that is relatively level, clear, clean, and dry. Sometimes, as you're paddling along near nightfall, this happy combination can seem practically nonexistent.

That was the feeling I had a few nights later, when I faced another commando camping challenge. I was paddling the stretch between Lechlade and Oxford where the river has no towns, and I had seen no sign of a B&B throughout the day. As the afternoon wore on, I began to grow anxious. I was battling blustery, chilly winds, and I had not seen any secluded bit of forest of the kind I needed for my campsite. At 5 p.m., I was pulling along the water toward the ancient stone arches of Newbridge (whenever you see the adjective "new" as part of a place name in England, be assured that the thing in question is as old as the hills—this particular Newbridge was built in 1250). My course took me near a group of people gathered at picnic tables on the lawn beside a pub. As I rounded the bend and headed toward the bridge, a man's voice called out, "Would you like a glass of wine?"

My first impulse was to decline, for two reasons: First, I hadn't found a place to stay, and I didn't want to use up precious daylight hours socializing before I'd settled this critical problem. Second, I don't drink wine because it usually leaves me sluggish, mentally and physically. So for many years I've refused offers of alcoholic drinks. I was just about to decline the invitation when I caught myself, and my right brain shouted, *What is traveling all about, for Pete's sake?! Travel means being open, taking risks, moving out of your comfort zone.* I realized right brain had a point. The world was reaching out to me, and it was my duty to take up the challenge, even if I did risk ending up homeless and hung over.

"Sure," I called back, and pulled to shore. It turned out that the pub was closed for the rest of the day, and this was a gathering of the staff, celebrating the departure of Rose, a recent college graduate who had won a competition for a post as buyer at a major department store chain. The man awarding me the glass of wine was the jovial pub owner. After introductions, I asked a question that had been puzzling me for days.

"Who owns the swans on the Thames?"

Everyone answered at once: "The Queen!"

"So if I was to take one . . . ?"

"You'd be locked in the Tower, son," said the pub owner.

"You'd be locked in the Tower and beheaded," he continued. "Seriously!" Everyone laughed.

One of the waitresses broke through the exclamations. "No he wouldn't," she said with authority. "It's treason, but not high treason." More laughter.

Turns out, everyone knew about the ownership of the swans because of the famous "swan upping" that takes place every year toward the end of July. In medieval times, swans were considered great eating, so monarchs like the gluttonous Henry VIII claimed them for the royal tables. To assert this claim, kings had their agents count and brand the swans, and this ancient practice is still carried out today. Royal officers, dressed in resplendent red uniforms, row up the river from Windsor in traditional wooden skiffs, with the mission of trapping and branding all the new cygnets and claiming them for the crown. This enterprise makes for delightful, splashing photo ops, as officers wrestle with adult swans angry at humans messing with their babies; but in the end, the redcoats, albeit a little wet and slightly embarrassed, win the battles.

"Does anybody eat swans?" I asked.

"Not today," was the reply. Apparently, in bird-loving England, even the queen wouldn't dare—even if she wanted to.

The pub owner said, "I've spent all of my life on the river, and I'm a swan catcher, and protector. . . ."

"Really?" I asked. "What do you do, just grab their neck?"

"Yah, yah."

"Don't they bite?"

"Nah, nah. They don't have any teeth. They just make a lot of noise"—he made a hissing sound—"but basically, they're stupid. You know what they're afraid of most in the world?"

"What?"

"Water. If you really want to get rid of them, splash them. I know it sounds stupid, but if you want to get rid of a swan, splash water at them. They're frightened of it." After describing several recent captures—one swan was trapped in a garage, another in a schoolyard—he summarized his knowledge.

"Two things to know about swans: One is they don't have teeth, and two is they're more frightened of you than you are of them. Once you catch them, they become extremely docile, and they just put their head way out"—pushing his arm far away from his body—"and they're no problem at all to deal with." Then he added in a jocular tone, "But we keep it a bit of a secret between those of us that know, so everybody thinks it's difficult."

During our chat, it came out that I was homeless and in need of a place to camp. Without missing a beat, the pub owner offered to let me camp on the pub's lawn.

During my conversation with Rose, I learned that she was facing a dilemma when she started her new job in London the following Monday. Her family had adopted three shelter dogs that were quite nervous and unruly, and needed to be watched. "They're chewing the furniture to bits!" she exclaimed. "It's terrible!" Until now, she had been able to take them out for a walk each day (her mom and dad both work outside the home). Now that she was moving to London, the family would need to make arrangements for a dog-sitter. They didn't want to put the dogs in a kennel because they felt that would be too stressful for them. I marveled at the lengths to which some compassionate people will go to rescue stray animals.

Rose's father Peter Walker arrived. He was president of an executive search company, and this gave me a chance to ask him about the inflated levels of compensation for high business executives. I was surprised to find that he immediately agreed that salaries were unreasonably high.

"The problem is," he said, "that the pool of possible applicants is so small. An ordinary person, even though he's intelligent, well educated and all, can't even be considered for such a position."

"Why not?"

"He has to have proven himself by being a top executive already. Remember, you're turning over to them the fate of an enterprise worth hundreds of millions of pounds." He took a sip of wine. "So it's a very exclusive group you're drawing from," he continued, "and they can get practically whatever they ask."

Our conversation turned to his daughter Rose, who was well on the way to becoming a top executive herself. He explained that the competition for the post she won had been very stiff, involving over 100 applicants. In his reserved way, he was quite proud of her.

Toward sunset the party broke up, with everyone saying good-bye, and I was left alone on the pub grounds, trying to locate a potential sleeping spot sheltered from the bitter wind. (I was cold most of the time on this kayak trip—morning, noon, and night; I rarely took off my sweater, even while paddling.) I found the least windy spot, on the leeward side of a tool shed, and sat with my back against it, huddling in my parka, disconsolately nibbling on the tasteless bits of beef jerky that were to be my supper.

Suddenly, I looked up and there were Peter and Rose, peeking at me from around the side of the shed. They had returned to invite me to come home with them for the night. I didn't spend much time pondering this astonishing good fortune, though to show my good breeding, I made a pro forma hesitation: "Well, if you're sure it wouldn't be imposing . . . ?"

During the drive to the Walker home, racing down the narrow, curvy one-lane paved tracks that constitute the British road system once off the highways, Peter suddenly remembered a point: "Oh, are you all right with dogs? We have three of them at the moment, and while they're harmless, they can be excitable."

"No problem," I said.

It then occurred to me that the reason I was in this car, being taken to a warm, affectionate English home, is that I, too, was a beneficiary of the Walker family's compassion for strays.

Once home, I met Jane, Peter's wife, and the four of us had a superb supper of Indian takeaway, which featured chicken tikka masala—an Indian dish that appears to be supplanting roast beef and Yorkshire pudding as the iconic English meal.

The dogs, by the way, seemed perfectly behaved, and I could see no evidence of the depredations Rose was concerned about. Later we moved into the beautifully kept living room—where the dogs were not allowed.

At bedtime, I was given the bedroom of the Walker's absent daughter, Helen.

I had the best sleep of the trip so far on her cloud-soft mattress and awoke the next morning feeling thoroughly refreshed. Enjoying a hot shower in her private suite, I reflected that perhaps that glass of wine I feared so much was not my enemy after all.

I paddled away from Newbridge the following morning feeling somewhat reassured about how English property owners would react to a homeless American kayaker. If the pub owner and the Walkers were any guide, I would not be treated harshly. Indeed, as the days passed, I failed to experience even one negative reaction to my intrusions. Several times during each day, I would leave the kayak on someone's property, either moored at a dock, left against a bank, or lifted onto the grass somewhere, and no one complained. And every night that I stayed in a B&B, I left my kayak somewhere along the bank, again without objection.

A week later, I saw a set of unusual signs pertaining to mooring rights, signs that implied a great deal about how the English might react to intrusions on private property. Instead of the usual "No Mooring" signs that one sees here and there along the river, these signs expressed the landowner's wishes in unexpected wording:

Sorry
No Mooring
Please

The more I thought about these signs—and when you're traveling on a slow-moving kayak, you have plenty of time to think about features you notice on shore—the more astonishing they seemed, for they revealed a striking level of courtesy. I tried to imagine the thought process that might have led to their production:

> *Horace:* Mildred dear, I think we'd better put up some "No Mooring" signs on the property we just purchased along the river.
> *Mildred:* But Darling, "No Mooring" sounds so hostile, so unfriendly. It makes us seem rude.

> *Horace:* Yes, I see your point. But I think we ought
> to express some kind of concern. Otherwise, the
> narrow boats will think they can stop there indefi-
> nitely and take it over.
> *Mildred:* But isn't there a nice way of saying it?
> *Horace:* I suppose we could say, "Sorry, no mooring."
> *Mildred:* Yes, that would be more polite. (*pause*)
> *Horace:* I see you're not convinced.
> *Mildred:* Well, couldn't it be a little more . . . I don't
> know . . . sensitive? We don't want to put anyone
> off.
> *Horace:* Well, I suppose we could add, "please."
> Then no one would consider us uncivil.
> *Mildred:* You're so clever!

Now of course, as I mentioned, these mooring signs were
unusual; statistically, they were outliers. But outliers help define
the location of the mean, and these signs clearly suggested that the
average level of social sensitivity in England falls strongly toward
the side of politeness.

Many other clues confirm this elevated level of courtesy. Several days after leaving Newbridge, I entered a crowded pub at sup-
pertime and, before my eyes adjusted to the dark, I walked right
into the back of a man who was standing there chatting with his
friends. I was the aggressor, entirely in the wrong, and I began to
formulate words to say in apology, but I was much too slow for
him. In a split second, he wheeled around and said, "Sorry"—and
it was a genuine, heartfelt apology.

Tone of voice is a clue to social sensitivity. Some years ago,
on an earlier trip to England, I was conversing with a young
woman in a pub who suggested some cultural differences between
Americans and the English. "Like what differences?" I asked.

Until that moment, I thought I was well on my way to making a good impression.

"Well, for one thing," she said, a slight edge of reproof in her voice, "Americans are louder."

The instant she said it, I realized with great mortification that she was absolutely right. I was speaking in a loud, booming tone that enabled every quietly conversing patron in the pub to mark me as a bumptious Yank. I was following a pattern the English have noted for generations. As far back as 1890, the English novelist Rudyard Kipling complained of "the Americans, whose rasping voices in the hush of a hot afternoon strain tense-drawn nerves to breaking-point."

Another clue about politeness comes from cell phone usage. In public places in England—streets, restaurants—you rarely see people openly chattering on cell phones, as is so common in another country I'm too polite to name. In groups of friends and acquaintances, cell phone use is rather carefully limited. Among the dozens of people I met in England, I never had a conversation interrupted by a cell phone call. Rose, Peter, and Jane were typical. They were busy people with complicated lives and they each had a cell phone ("mobile" as the English say), but I never saw them using it. They discreetly excused themselves to take care of business.

The famous, reserved manner of the English is also an outgrowth of politeness; it does not spring from coldness or indifference, as it might seem at first. My experience wrestling my humongous kayak pack in the trains that took me from Heathrow Airport to Cricklade gave me a feel for this fascinating mixture of sympathy and reserve. My struggles prompted many looks of concern, but onlookers hesitated to offer to help. One reason for their hesitation, I think, was to avoid insulting me: An offer to help would imply that I appeared to be incapable of carrying my own luggage.

At Swindon, where I completed my train journey, I experienced a practical gauge of the social concern that surrounded me. I half lifted, half dragged the kayak from the railroad car onto the platform, and then sat down on the concrete to wriggle into the arm straps of the pack. Seeing me on the pavement, three people rushed up to help me, thinking I had fallen down. One of them, a young man no bigger than me, insisted on carrying the pack out of the station to my taxi.

If you want to see what's behind English reserve, just ask directions in an English town and you'll see what I'm talking about. A person who seems aloof—careful not to make eye contact or exhibit interest in your affairs—will, once asked for aid, become unstoppably helpful, tying herself in knots trying to give directions for getting from here to there on complicated English streets.

So as the days passed, I became less and less concerned about hostile responses to my commando camping. I had increasing confidence that if they noticed me camping on their property, Horace and Mildred would not be the kind of people to pull out a shotgun. My thinking shifted more to the thought that *I* was being discourteous by making these intrusions, and that I had a duty to keep them as unobtrusive as possible. I was becoming English!

Seeing that astonishingly polite sign about trespassing on the Thames put me in mind of the most astonishingly *impolite* "No Trespassing" sign I have ever seen. I came across it while gold panning along the south fork of the Clearwater River in Idaho:

Is There Life after Death?
Trespass and Find Out!

Of course, this sign was an extreme example, an outlier, but like the English outlier, it indicated something about the average tendency of the culture. It said that Americans are not so concerned about offending strangers, that in their quest for a good laugh, Americans are willing to risk seeming rude. Driven by curiosity to find out who might have put up such a droll sign, I went up the forbidden Idaho road to see what stood at the end of it. I did not on this occasion discover eternity. Instead, I found a crew of four men who were struggling to resurrect a defunct gold mine, and who found a stranger's arrival a welcome excuse to break for a convivial round of doughnuts and coffee.

3
The Lockside Community

The guidebooks say the Thames is spanned by 214 bridges; at the Gloucestershire village of Lechlade-on-Thames, I came upon a fine example of one—the Ha'Penny Bridge. Built in 1792—and in those days charging a toll of a half penny—this bridge spans the river in a single low arch. It's made of tightly fitting blocks of a type of yellow stone that rainwater has turned black with lichen's stains. I spent some time paddling beneath it, camera in hand, striving to capture it perfectly, framed amid swans and the long, trailing boughs of the weeping willows.

Standing a half mile downriver from Lechlade is St. John's Lock, the first of the 44 locks on the Thames. The locks are owned and run by a government bureaucracy, the Environment Agency, a fact that led me to expect trouble as I approached St. John's Lock. One worry was the question of my license—or rather, my lack of one.

I had read that licenses are required of every craft on the Thames, but I am not the kind of person who, when hearing of a government requirement about something, eagerly leaps to conform to it. As a matter of fact, it rather stuck in my craw that a kayaker would have to apply to a government to get permission to paddle on one of God's rivers. *What's next*, I thought, *a permit to smell flowers?* So I didn't have a license, and had already illegally paddled 14 miles on the Thames. Now I was about to meet "the man," a government official who might chastise me or even fine

me for my lack of cooperation—in addition to ordering me to pur-
chase the deplored license.

My attitude toward waterborne authority has a long, unhappy
history. On my home waters, Lake Pend Oreille in northern Idaho,
the Bonner County sheriff has six patrol boats, whose officers
apparently have nothing to do all day but pester boaters, including
paddlers, about maritime regulations. Once, when my wife Judy
and I were out in the canoe near sunset and didn't have a flash-
light, the officer insisted we leave the lake and "escorted" us all the
way back to the marina while the whole world watched.

So as I approached St. John's Lock and prepared to meet the
government official in charge of it, I knew there was a potential
for hard feelings and heated words. I put on my life jacket, which
I almost never wear, hoping this would ingratiate me with officialdom. I tied up the kayak above the gates, and walked to the
lock area to see what was in store. The lockkeeper came toward
me from the other end—he had been trimming a hedge in the
lock house garden. He was a short man of slight build with rather
unruly hair. He wasn't wearing any uniform or badge, a fact that
I found mildly encouraging. The only garment that suggested
his official status was a red rubber life jacket, but—a point that
seemed significant—it was uninflated, hanging uselessly over his
shoulders. I sensed that he was obeying the letter of some regula-
tion applying to lockkeepers, but not its spirit—a strong clue that
he might be a kindred soul.

"Are you wanting to lock through?" he asked with a friendly
smile on his face. There was not a trace of demand or authority in
his voice. I explained that was my desire.

"Where are you from?" he asked picking up on my American
accent.

I explained about my journey, and in minutes, David and I were friends.

In the course of the conversation, he asked, "Have you got the license for the boat?" He wasn't demanding I get one. He spoke as if this was a requirement imposed by nature, like the need for an umbrella against rain, and he could do me a favor by supplying it.

We went to the lockkeeper's office where he pulled out the regulations, and together we examined the formula for working out the cost. It was up to me to declare the size of the boat and the time I wanted to be on the river; he would issue the category of license I wanted. I decided I would truthfully declare a 12-foot kayak for one month, and he worked out the cost to be £15, an amount I happily paid. Thinking it over, I decided that this charge shouldn't be considered a license; it was really a user fee that paid for the construction and maintenance of the locks, and for the lockkeepers (who, in addition to working the locks, are responsible for maintaining the grounds and the beautiful lock house gardens).

Some minutes later, David had worked the sluices and gates, and I was sitting on my kayak in the middle of the lock—the only boat there—as the water level started to fall.

"Could you take a picture of me, so I can show my friends?" I asked.

He agreed, and I passed the camera up to him. He busied himself taking shots from different spots on the lock. When he handed it back, he said, "I got a real good picture of you with the church tower in the background. I think you'll like it."

Soon the lock emptied. As I glided out between the massive gates, I gave him a hearty "Thank you."

"Have a good trip," he said and waved good-bye.

As I learned on subsequent days, David was not an exception. The lockkeepers all the way down the Thames were friendly—and relaxed. For example, though the lockkeepers themselves wear life jackets—the same uninflated red kind that David had—they don't hound anyone going through the locks about wearing them (virtually all boaters don't).

The positive energy surrounding the locks goes beyond the helpfulness of the lockkeepers. Something rather magical happens at the locks, and everyone there—boat crews, boat passengers, and spectators—shares in it. As I traversed the locks, one by one, I began to grasp the elements that make up this atmosphere of healthy camaraderie.

Locks are big, exciting machines that bring out the kid in all of us. They have huge wooden gates that swing open and then close with an earth-shaking thud. At the manually operated locks, you open the gates by throwing all your weight against the end of a long wooden beam. On the electrically powered lock gates, you push a little chrome button on the control panel, hear the clunk of the solenoid engaging, and watch tons of wood majestically part. Locks also have sluice gates that you open, releasing a boiling cascade of water into the deep lock below. The fruit of this complicated labor is an amazing result: Mighty boats—and little kayaks too—rise gently into the sunshine. This entire system is a delight to watch, a giant kinetic sculpture that attracts tourists and passersby who lean over, peer, photograph, and wave. Indeed, so distinctive is this pastime of canal-side watching that the English have a special word for the person who does it. He is a *gongoozler* (the word derived from dialect terms meaning stare and gape).

The lock's machinery is, to a degree, dangerous: A person could get crushed, a boat could be overturned, a child could tumble into the chasm of water. Normally in our society, big, dangerous machines are sealed away from the public by high fences. Specially certified people are given the exclusive right to operate them, and it is a crime, or at least some kind of industrial violation, for an ordinary person to touch the controls. As a result of this exclusivity, the people operating the machines become rather self-important. At first, I couldn't figure out why this doesn't happen at the English locks, why the lockkeepers don't become aloof and superior.

The answer became clear to me on a later day when I approached Clifton Lock, below Abingdon, rather late one evening. There was no one at the lock, and a little round sign at the head of the lock said "SELF-SERVICE." I hadn't noticed it before, but these flip-down signs stand at every lock, enabling the lockkeeper to announce the self-service condition when he goes for his one-hour lunch break, and also from the time he quits at 6 p.m. until he returns the next morning at 9 a.m. It was up to me to work the lock that evening by myself if I wanted to continue on my journey. That was, of course, a challenge the kid in me was delighted to accept.

Over the ensuing days, I came to see how this self-service arrangement democratizes the locks. The fact that anybody and everybody can run the locks entirely changes the social dynamics. The lockkeeper cannot project the idea that he is the only person capable of operating the lock, and the only person permitted by authority to do so. Therefore, he doesn't adopt a stance of superiority. At the locks, we are equals.

I had a little fun at a lock one evening a few days later. After putting my kayak through, I spied two narrowboats coming down the river. Knowing they would need passage, I decided to tarry and take up the job of being their lockkeeper. At the time of my trip, England was going through a period of fiscal austerity, and the government had announced layoffs in many areas. Lockkeepers of the Environment Agency were among the positions where cuts were being discussed.

I got to work opening and closing the necessary sluices, and when the lock had filled, I pushed open the gate and waved them in.

"Hello, Hello," I sang out like I owned the place. Then I spread my arms wide and with an official tone in my voice, I boomed out, "Welcome to the lock."

The crews were amused by my playacting, but I could see from their quizzical looks that they had picked up on my accent, and knew something didn't compute.

"I'm part of the group that's been sent over here from America to operate the locks," I told them. "It's part of the austerity program." They got a good laugh out of that.

My jest underscored the elementary reality that everyone is a lockkeeper. This applies not just to boat crews, but also to spectators who may live in nearby residences, and hikers walking along the Thames Path (which parallels the river all the way down). Many of these bystanders are eager to operate the lock for the benefit of boaters when the lockkeeper isn't present; they obviously get a kick out of controlling this massive machinery.

So what has been created at the lock is a community of equals who serve one another—and who are grateful to one another. The lockkeeper is included in this aura of gratitude. Yes, he is an employee and he is required to do his job. But we as boaters know that this job of opening and closing gates and sluices is also *our* job, the job that we would have to do if he didn't happen to be there. So when we say, "Thank you" to the lockkeeper after passing through, there is real sincerity in our words.

The spirit of democracy that prevails at the locks may be a rather recent development, brought about by the modern need to limit lockkeepers' working hours. In earlier times, lockkeepers were in charge of the locks 24 hours a day, and could be woken up at 2 a.m. to let a boat through. One report on Boulters Lock at Maidenhead mentioned that on a busy day in 1904, the lockkeeper "was on duty from 5 a.m. to 11 p.m., and had no time for meals." Having full control of the machinery, the lockkeeper was not a friendly equal, but rose to a position of authority. "He ruled as the most just and benevolent of dictators," the admiring historian said of this Boulters lockkeeper, "and his firm commands, sometimes spiced with irony or sarcasm when occasion warranted, enforced obedience."

Personally, I'd rather encounter a friendly lockkeeper.

An hour after leaving St. John's Lock, having traveled three miles down the river, I came to Kelmscott Manor, the country estate belonging to William Morris. According to the thumbnail sketch of him, Morris was a 19th-century "writer, designer, and socialist," and it was this last tag—socialist—that prompted me to visit the estate. I had just written a book about the beliefs that bring people to socialism, and I was curious to see if Morris fit my theories. I was in for a surprise. I discovered that William Morris was an astonishingly original thinker who propounded many thought-provoking ideas, ideas worth considering even if we cannot see how to implement them today.

I soon concluded that Morris should probably not be considered a socialist at all. The cornerstone of modern socialist ideology, faith in government as society's problem solver, had no part in Morris's thinking. In his 1890 utopian novella, *News from Nowhere*, Morris paints a society where there is no government, and people operate successfully in small, friendly communities without any overarching authority to tell them what to do.

Morris believed that workers in these local communities would express their art in practical and unembellished buildings. He bought Kelmscott because it fit this model. It is a rather plain 16th-century farmhouse with an authentic, functional feel. The roofs of the buildings are especially noteworthy. In England, something hard and graceful covers roofs, usually slate, artificial slate, or red ceramic tiles. But Kelmscott has none of these. Instead, the roofs are covered with fat, lichen-encrusted granite stones. This type of stone roof is not uncommon in Gloucestershire. Nearly half the buildings in Lechlade had them. At one old building in town that was being completely rebuilt, the ancient stones of the roof were neatly stacked to one side, ready to be put on after the new roof rafters were installed.

I joined a small group of tourists at the main entrance to the farmhouse, and we were taken in hand by a volunteer docent. Morris, she pointed out, was independently wealthy, but chose to work—an unusual career move in 19th-century England where idleness was a mark of status, and rolling up one's shirtsleeves was generally taken as a sign of unfortunate social decline. Morris didn't just work; he worked hard, plunging into many crafts and businesses including printing, ceramics, and interior decoration. One of his specialties was designing textiles, and having a quilting-mad spouse, I made a mental note to buy some fabric of his "Strawberry Thief" design for her when I reached London.

In *News from Nowhere*, Morris postulates a future that rejects standard economic principles. In a coincidence that echoed my trip, the hero of the story makes a trip along the River Thames with his new acquaintances. The boating party—in two skiffs—visits communities on the river, finding in each a contented, self-sufficient social order. One thing the narrator discovers in this new regime is that everyone enjoys work. In Morris's future, no one works for money; in fact, there is no money in this advanced society. Instead, all the jobs that need to be done—sowing, reaping, shoemaking, weaving, and so on—are undertaken for the pleasure of participating, creating, and contributing to others. This idea that people would work simply for the satisfaction of it did fit Morris himself, of course. So you could say that he lived his philosophy. But as a formula for an entire economic system, it seemed rather far-fetched when I first heard the docent at Kelmscott describe it.

Another of the mind-stretching ideas Morris advanced was the view that we should turn our backs on the efficiency of modern methods of production. He felt that factories, machines, and modern energy systems involving coal, oil, and electricity were debasing human existence, turning us into machines ourselves. We should return, he said, to the more primitive methods of creating goods and services, working with our hands, directly controlling our product and establishing personal relationships with the human beings in our environment. Utopia, for Morris, was a world founded upon human connections made possible through local arts and crafts.

Although a highly appealing image, it seemed quite unrealistic. Logic seemed to dictate that if you returned to primitive methods of production, then you would get primitive standards of living.

Surely, I thought, the history of the human race from the days of fire and that first wheel is the story of increasing the efficiency of production to improve standards of living. Do away with machines, and mankind retrogresses to the Stone Age.

At least that was my first reaction. But after I walked out of the house into the sunlight, and set out on the footpath back to my kayak on the river, I began to see another angle. I began to see that I, of all people, shouldn't be criticizing Morris's philosophy, since I was actually living it! Consider this: From Cricklade, the English village where the River Thames became deep enough to accommodate my kayak, to North Woolwich, the London docklands suburb where I pulled the boat out of the river, the distance is 170 miles on the twisting river, and 80 miles as the crow flies. In a sleek, steel tour bus powered by a petroleum distillate, this distance could be traveled in two to three hours—assuming no traffic holdups. In my faded red canvas kayak powered by not-very-impressive pectoral muscles, I made the trip in 29 days.

I was finding that traversing the heart of England by the method of the Inuit peoples deeply rewarding, bringing me into more meaningful contact with people and places than industrial tourism would have permitted. Furthermore, much of what I encountered in this relaxed journey yielded deeper lessons. When patiently regarded, the world suggests larger truths running below the surface—truths we can perhaps touch with the tips of our fingers, but not grasp and pack away in a box.

I began to see that Morris's idea might have some validity, and that the world needs to reconsider its relentless quest for industrial efficiency. I haven't decided exactly how far we should go in turning our backs on modern technology. I did, after all, rely on a big, modern machine powered by a petroleum distillate to get me and my kayak to England. But I know that my slow and digressive progress down the Thames was a richly rewarding experience.

It also occurred to me that behavior at the locks supported another of Morris's ideas, the idea that people don't need to be paid to work. When the spectators pitch in to do the work of opening gates and sluices, they are not given any type of money—not pound notes, or colored beads, or sacks of corn—in exchange for their labor. Their motive is the thrill of operating the locks and the pleasure of serving others.

So maybe Morris was on to something: Maybe people *can* be motivated to do work by the pleasure of it. That's an exhilarating idea, and it made me wonder if the human race might be happier if we figured out how to apply this principle more widely in the modern world, turning what we now call work into play.

4
The Parish Church

Whang! Whang! Whang! Whang! The hoarse clang of church bells, a mere 80 yards from the window of my hotel room, banished any possibility of enjoying a few moments of rest after a day on the water. It was early Friday evening in Lechlade, three days into my trip. Many tourists would suppose that these pealing bells were calling worshippers to an evening service, but I knew better. Back in 1992, when my wife Judy and I lived in a village in Devon, I had been a member of the bell-ringing band at the local church. I recognized this early evening ringing as a practice session, and I wanted to learn more about it. I leaped from the bed, made my way to the church tower, and crept up the narrow, winding stone stairway until I came to a little trap door. There I waited patiently until the ringing paused, and then I tapped at the panel above my head. The trap door was lifted. "Could an American visitor come up and watch what you're doing?" I asked.

"Of course, of course. Come right up," several people said at once.

When I'd clambered into the loft, I asked, "Would it be all right to take a few pictures?"

"That'll cost you extra," said one of the men, and we all laughed.

In the room I found ten people. Six men and women had just finished pulling on the ropes of the six bells, and four others, observers and apprentices, were seated on a narrow bench to the side, their feet carefully pulled back under the bench to stay clear of the long ends of the bell ropes. I was introduced to Maureen, the tower captain. During the break in practice, she announced the upcoming commitments, including ringing for a wedding that was to take place the following Saturday.

For a quaint and distinctive activity, you could hardly do better than this English custom of bell ringing. All over England, in thousands of church towers—3,067 to be exact—people of all ages and from all walks of life gather to manipulate these massive hunks of bronze. It's not music making in any ordinary sense. Nobody is following written notes, and even when the number of bells is large enough to complete a scale—say 8 to 12—no one ever attempts to play a song on the bells. Instead, what the band in the tower at Lechlade was doing in the first part of the practice was "rounds." This is ringing the bells in order, from highest to lowest, over and over. When the group had decided which person would pull which rope, everyone fell silent and looked upward at the six ropes coming through little holes in the ceiling high above.

"Tenor's going," said the man in control of the highest bell. He meant he was starting to pull.

About two seconds later he said, "Tenor's gone." This meant that the tenor bell, which had been balanced upside down, was now falling of its own weight, and that the other ringers could start timing their pulls accordingly.

If you had to place bell ringing in a category, I think it should be called a sport, an exercise of athletic coordination. It is unusual, however, in that the players do not compete against one another, but rather work together to overcome physics. The objective of the ringers—assuming they have mastered the order in which the bells need to be rung—is to ring the bells evenly. This is a difficult challenge.

The bell at rest is perched exactly upside down. To make it strike, the ringer pulls on the rope to make it start to fall, like the Leaning Tower of Pisa finally succumbing to the pull of gravity. Some few seconds after that pull, the bell will rotate down to the bottom of its arc, at which point the clapper will flop over and produce the desired clang. Then the bell continues rotating until it has gone full circle and ends perched upside down and motionless, waiting to be pulled again.

Because there's a delay between the pull on the rope and the clang of the bell, everybody must employ a great deal of anticipation to make the bells strike evenly. When beginners are at work, the bells sound quite jerky and irregular. When experts ring the bells, the cadence is not only even, but also fast! I'll never forget how astonished I was when I first heard the bells of St. Martins-in-the-Fields in London. The ringers were moving the 12 bells at a pace twice that of an ordinary tower, producing a deafening blur of sound echoing and re-echoing from the stone buildings on Trafalgar Square.

After the Lechlade group had practiced rounds, they began to work on "method ringing." Methods are preset systems that rotate the sequence in which the bells are rung so that, eventually, all combinations in the order of the bells have sounded. To play out all these combinations and permutations in a complete peal can take many hours, even with a six- or eight-bell ring, so they are rarely attempted in their entirety. The beginning level of method ringing is the "plain hunt," and after a year of trying, I almost mastered that at the Devon church where I rang 20 years ago. Beyond this elementary level, there are methods whose very names signal their hair-curling complexity, including Stedman Triples, Reverse Canterbury, and Double Bob Maximus.

The Lechlade band's efforts at method ringing were creditable, but on one occasion the rhythm of the bells faltered, as one ringer lost his place, throwing the following ringers off their timing. Two bells started to strike together, then the ringing collapsed into a jumbled smashup with all the bells ringing nearly at once, sounding very much like a series of repeated car crashes. Maureen shouted, "Stand!" and the ringers pulled their bells to the top and left them there, silent. Then they exchanged guilty smiles of embarrassment, knowing that the whole town had heard their spectacular boo-boo.

Although bell ringing does take place in other countries, it is a distinctively English activity. England has, as I noted, 3,067 functioning towers with active bands; the rest of the world has 256 (the United States has 33, including one at the Old Post Office Tower in Washington, DC). Naturally, the bell-ringing community is concerned with maintaining interest in its "sport" and seeks to recruit new participants, especially among the young. One impediment to attracting youngsters, reports the Central Council of Church Bell Ringers, is the recent passage of the Children's Protection Act. There is some danger connected with bell ringing, especially the possibility that one might entangle a limb in the bell rope, and have it jerked up by the force of the moving bell. Although it's not clear what the Children's Protection Act forbids or requires, or how it applies to bell ringing, it has prompted some towers to restrict the participation of youngsters.

I was pleased to see that they did have one young ringer in Lechlade, a slight girl of about 10, Maureen's daughter. She was so short that she had to stand on a special wooden platform they had made for her. She was given the treble bell to operate, which is the lightest one, although still hundreds of pounds of metal. I took a picture of her pulling on the bell rope, a look of intense concentration on her face, radiating pride at joining the adults in such a challenging task.

When the practice was over, everyone slowly and carefully descended the narrow stairway and emerged from the church into the rays of the setting sun. The ringers headed for their homes, but I tarried, attracted by the parish churchyard and its spread of tipping, slanting tombstones of long-departed parishioners. I inspected these with great interest to discern what I could about their lives, and to see how far back they dated. I found, however, that most of the stones were unreadable. Most were cut from a local honey-colored limestone that weathered rather rapidly, so that, after what I guessed to be about 200 years, all inscriptions had disappeared. They were not without "writing" however, because a species of lichen had grown across their faces in a distinctive pattern—a pattern repeated on stone after stone. This image rattled around in my head for many days afterward, until it emerged as a poem.

In a Parish Churchyard

Dark yews o'ershadow ancient stones
—All canted, never square—
Telling naught of nameless dead,
Their faces too eraséd to be read.
Showing now in lichen's inky vein
That men of every fame all read the same.

5
Dramatis Personae

England is a windy land, a not surprising consequence of being an island in the middle of a stormy sea. On the Thames, there aren't any significant waves, for the water is too narrow, but the wind, if coming head on, can provide a challenge to a kayaker. My folding kayak, a Klepper Aerius, is high and wide. That makes it difficult to tip over—a feature that has probably saved my life in more than one crisis—but its big, boxy cross-section means that it hates a headwind.

On the morning after leaving the Walker family at Newbridge, I had to grapple with a stiff southerly breeze, a 30 mph blast that made the trees overhead surge and roar, and that pinned my ears back when I turned to face it. It also tore off my cap, which meant I had to stow it and paddle with my head uncovered against the sun. My destination that day was Oxford, 12 miles away. From Newbridge, the river runs northeast, so the wind initially tended to be a benefit, speeding me along my way. However, after a look at the map, I knew that the free ride would not last. After heading northeast for eight miles, the river veers sharply at King's Lock and heads south into Oxford—leaving me to paddle straight into that gushing blast of air.

Long before I reached that turn, I had been given a taste of what this headwind would mean. Occasionally, the river would make one of its meandering turns and force me to battle directly against the wind for a few hundred yards. Each episode was an exhausting struggle. I could not stop paddling even for a few seconds, for the wind would drive the boat back, erasing in moments the few feet of forward progress I had wrested from the river. One trick I employed was to nose the boat behind clumps of trees and segments of high bank that helped break the force of the wind. When I needed a rest, I would find a willow branch to hold on to, so as not to lose any forward progress. These techniques, combined with furious, calorie-draining paddling, enabled me to travel against this wind, but at a rate of about two-tenths of a mile per hour.

I reached King's Lock in the early afternoon, made the turn into the wind and, inch by inch, clawed my way a half mile to Godstow Lock. I concluded it was pointless for me to attempt to go farther. I tied the kayak to a tree branch and disembarked to explore my options.

I had landed in a very public area, with two roads crossing the river and a footpath alongside it—a footpath heavily used by Oxford students on their bicycles and by hard-driving joggers. In addition, this was a mooring area for canal boats. As a camping spot, it was unacceptable: Even a homeless person feels embarrassed trying to sleep in front of the whole world. The only alternative seemed to be to stash the kayak somewhere around the lock area, find a bus into Oxford, and get a hotel room there. I could come back for the boat in a day or two, when the wind had abated.

I approached a man standing on a narrowboat to ask for advice about whether the area was safe for leaving the kayak. His first reaction was that it would not be a good idea. "Where are you heading, anyway?" he asked.

"I'm trying to get to Oxford, but I can't go against this wind."

"I have an idea that may work, if you don't mind waiting a bit."

He explained that he was with a group headed into Oxford on the narrowboat. The rest of the party had repaired to a nearby pub for refreshment, leaving him to watch the boat. He suggested that my kayak could be hoisted onto the top of the boat and I could travel to Oxford with them. Because the alternative was a seeming eternity of life-draining paddling, I didn't even pretend to hesitate over his offer.

Ian's craft was a typical narrowboat, a little over 6 feet wide and about 60 feet long. These boats dominate the waters of the Thames. They were originally cargo vessels, made to fit the narrow locks of the country's vast network of canals. Nowadays, they are leisure crafts—usually rented by the week, or for a weekend—and have all the amenities, including beds, stove, and shower located on either side of the single central aisle. They are painted in conservative colors, reminiscent of their coal-carrying ancestry: dark green, dark red, or, as was the case with Ian's craft, dark blue with light-yellow trim. They travel very slowly, around 5 mph, which is a good thing since they are, in many cases, commanded by customers who have never touched a tiller before.

Soon the passengers, a group of older men and women, came back from the pub in a cheery and talkative mood. My kayak was quickly hoisted onto the top of the boat, tied down with a rope, and I was invited to enter the cabin. It turned out that I had joined a birthday party, and a reunion of old friends. The group had formed originally when the members were patrons of a pub in Buckinghamshire; even though many of them had moved away from the original locale, they still kept in touch. Ian had rented this boat so they could spend the day together, and in the process celebrate the birthday of one of the men. The boat was following a loop along the Oxford Canal and the Thames, ending back at the starting point that evening. Since Ian had rented the boat, he felt responsible for it. He insisted on doing all the driving, seated in the cockpit at the rear, holding the long tiller handle, his anorak zipped against the wind. After a few minutes, the novelty of watching him steer wore off, and I left him to his lonely post. Being careful to duck under the low rear doorway, I went down three tiny steps into the warmth of the cabins below.

Below decks, a narrowboat is cozy, but perhaps too cozy for a large group. The center aisle is very narrow, about three inches tighter than the aisle in airplane economy class, so there's not much mingling possible. Most of us found seats in one of the two open sections, and allowed two industrious (and slender) ladies to slip up and down the aisle serving us ham sandwiches, crisps (chips), and drinks (yes, I tried a glass of wine, again without ill effect). A few people asked about my background, but they were mainly interested in their old friends, chatting and giggling exuberantly about old times. Much of the humor seemed to involve wink-wink, nudge-nudge episodes. With my one glass of wine, I hadn't quite caught up to their ethanol level, and I adopted the role of friendly observer.

Ian had taken me under his wing to a greater degree than I realized. While I tippled below, he was using his mobile phone to contact the lockkeeper at Osney Lock in Oxford, to arrange a safe place to leave my boat. And it worked out perfectly. In the heart of Oxford, Ian pulled the boat to the bank, and I said goodbye to the birthday boy—an airline pilot nearing retirement—and his mates and jolly girlfriends. Several of the men gently lifted the kayak from the top of the narrowboat, and I was back on the river again.

In a few moments, I reached Osney Lock, and Peter, the lockkeeper, showed me a special dock belonging to the Environment Agency where I could moor the boat in relative safety while I toured Oxford for the next days. I expect it was against the rules of the Agency to allow that, but lockkeepers instinctively put the interests of humanity above those of bureaucracy.

Oxford was the first city on my route, the first place on the Thames that had tall buildings, double-decked buses, a railroad station, and banks with plate-glass windows. It also had bicycles . . . a swarm of bicycles. At the railroad station, a half-acre parking lot was crammed with hundreds of cycles that commuters had left for the day. At intersections, bicyclists crowded in a clump waiting for the light to change. It all seemed so terribly dangerous, the wheeled humans mixing among the lines of cars and darting in front of giant buses and lorries that lumbered along like blinded elephants.

Unwheeled humans—the pedestrians—faced similar dangers, and especially if they were Americans who expected cars to be coming from the left when they stepped off the curb. Years ago, the American wife of a dear friend was killed by walking in front of a London bus. We suspected that she stepped off the curb looking the other way. So I didn't trust myself on the streets of Oxford. Every time I needed to cross, I would swivel my head from side to side, over and over, like a frightened squirrel, never feeling it was safe to proceed.

As if the traffic weren't enough of a distraction, there were on all sides amazing buildings to attract the gawker's attention. In art and architecture, Oxford is a treasure, reflecting centuries of human creativity at the highest level. The point was perhaps made best by an Italian tourist whom I overheard as he was leaving— and I entering—the Ashmolean Museum: *"Quanta cultura!"* he told his friend, shaking his head in disbelief. I think he was referring to the vast collection of paintings, sculpture, and artifacts in the museum, but it applied to the entire city as well. You cannot take a step without seeing an ornate staircase, railing, or window sill— not to mention a building or statue—that reflects tasteful, concentrated, artistic energy. So much culture!

Perhaps my favorite structure from among the scores of treasures in the city was the so-called Bridge of Sighs, a highly ornamented enclosed footbridge at Hertford College that arches over the street at the second-story level. As I looked into the bridge's background, I learned that just about everything popularly believed about it is charmingly false. It got its name for being a copy of a bridge in Venice, which it doesn't resemble at all. That Venice bridge, in turn, was given the name "Bridge of Sighs" not by the Venetians, but by the English poet Lord Byron, who supposed that condemned criminals used it when going to their deaths, heaving one last sigh at the sight of the world they were to leave forever. Actually, the jail with the bridge held petty criminals not to be executed. Even its appearance is a fraud. Its ornamented, classical look makes you think it was built in antiquity. In fact, it's one of those Victorian imitations that so irritate the martinets of modern architecture, and was built in 1914. Because its year of construction places it after the Victorian age, I suppose it should be called faux Victorian, making it a delightful imitation of an imitation.

The 38 colleges of the university constitute the soul of Oxford, each a repository of culture in itself. In one of these colleges, University College—the oldest, founded in 1249—I saw a performance of a play that was so remarkably well done that it prompted me to ponder the place of drama in English culture. The piece was Nikolai Gogol's *The Government Inspector*, a satirical comedy about local officials who learn that an inspector from Moscow, traveling incognito, is due to visit their town—and he will be bound to discover all their peccadilloes when he looks into their agencies. In their anxiety, the officials mistake a penniless drifter for the inspector, and they bend over backward to entertain, flatter, and bribe him. The play was put on entirely by the students, led by a student director, and rehearsed in a matter of weeks at the end of the spring term while the students were also studying for exams. It was staged in the Master's Garden, a wide expanse of lawn within the college precincts. There was no stage, no curtain, and no set—just a couch and a table set upon the grass. The students had erected some flood lamps to light the area for the second act after dark.

Despite these limitations and disadvantages—including airplanes flying overhead and birds tweeting in the shrubs along the Master's Garden wall—these kids utterly convinced me that they were Russian village officials with a vexing problem on their hands. They never seemed to miss a line—which means that when they did miss a line, they were so fully in character the audience couldn't detect it. These 20-year-olds were virtually professional actors! Such talent could have been explained had they been chosen as the winners of a nationwide acting contest. But because they were drawn from the student body of this little—500-student—college, I couldn't avoid the speculation that acting talent, and interest in drama, runs broad and deep in England.

Other clues support this suspicion. One is the pantomime tradition. In the Christmas–New Year season, in towns all over England, amateur actors leap upon the stage to perform comic tales. The hallmark of this tradition is overacting, getting ridiculously deep into parts of *Snow White, Cinderella,* and so on, playing villains and imperious matrons in drag. My wife Judy and I saw several amateur pantomimes given in Exmouth, Devon, when we lived there in 1992. They were unusual in their spontaneity, as if put together with a few phone calls.

Pageants and dramatic festivals have long been an important part of the English scene. Along the Thames, especially during the summer, locals plunge into theatrical productions. In the 19th century, one popular form of entertainment was the *tableaux vivants* (living scenes)—short skits of dramatic moments. These ranged from comedy—"Tea and Scandal"—to tongue-in-cheek melodrama—"Prince Charles' Farewell to Flora Macdonald," to the patriotic and tragic, such as "The Last Stand," an 1894 battle scene in China that depicts the celebrated Major Wilson and his men perishing while singing the national anthem.

Early in my trip down the Thames, at Lechlade, I came across one of these pageants, given on the grounds of a local pub. The tableau marked the 800th anniversary of the town being granted a royal charter as a market town. An extravagantly attired king read the proclamation, while his queen, also dressed in magnificent royal robes, stood at his side, regally resting her hand on his arm. Off to one side was Father Thames, a large, heavy-set man dressed in an opulent blue velvet robe, armed with a trident, seated on his throne. This tableau was followed by an outpouring of local talent, including children dancing, a band, an adult choir, and an orchestra composed entirely of recorders (the bass recorder was the size of a small telephone pole).

In attempting to explain the English keenness for acting, I pose one theory, that the English are not so affected by stage fright. After all, when you're self-conscious and embarrassed, it's not possible to confidently adopt a character. I formed this idea during church services we attended when Judy and I lived in Exmouth. One feature of the service, which our U.S. church also employs, was a children's time. During this time, the children come down to the front of the church, and the leader—usually the pastor—goes over some point in the scripture reading. In England, however, I noticed that these exchanges were quite candid and informal, with the leader freely and frankly chiding the children for some error in front of the entire congregation. For example, the exchange might run like this:

> *Priest:* Why do you think Jesus asked his disciples this question?
> *Boy:* (*in firm voice*): Because he didn't know the answer?
> *Priest:* (*good-naturedly*): What a silly thing to say! Of course he knew the answer. No, what was his real reason? Think.

I had never seen a frank exchange like that in any children's time back in the States. I think the reason is that American children are more likely to be shy, feeling embarrassed to be in front of the church congregation at all. Questions in the States tend to be rhetorical, because the children are usually silent, perhaps afraid to offer answers. If a child does say something, he mumbles in a hesitant voice, and the leader feels impelled to reassure him, and praise his contribution no matter how false or irrelevant. Correcting the children in front of an audience is considered too harsh a treatment for the self-conscious U.S. tots.

In general, it seems, English children are not so fearful about being in front of an audience. In fact, I suspect many of them rather like it. They, along with adults, have a certain "social confidence," a lack of anxiety about losing face in public. When you have that kind of thick social skin, you have the makings of being an actor. The English priest who was criticizing the boy was not embarrassing him; he was one actor "playing" to another—and they both enjoyed it.

The full force of the English enthusiasm for the stage hit me at the end of my journey when I became a tourist in London and turned to the project of selecting plays to see. It proved to be a bewildering challenge, because London is overflowing with drama, outpacing, I believe, any city in the world in this regard. Compare it with New York City, the drama capital of the United States, taking the data from the summer of 2011. For productions in large, centrally located theaters ("West End" in London, "Broadway" in New York), London had 116 (musicals, comedies, and dramas combined); New York had 36. For productions in small theaters away from the downtown center ("Fringe" in London, "Off Broadway" in New York), London had 102; New York had 37.

Pointing to the size of the potential audience strengthens this 3-to-1 ratio. New York draws upon a national population of 300 million, not to mention foreign visitors. London, by comparison, serves as the drama hub for a country of only 60 million, plus foreign visitors.

Other points confirm this affinity of the English for the stage. The longest-running play in the world is in London: Agatha Christie's murder mystery *The Mousetrap*, at St Martin's Theatre. The first performance was given in 1952, and the play entered its 59th year in 2011. The play has featured 382 actors for its eight roles; on average, the actors in it play their parts for over a year before moving on.

The number of theatrical productions is a function of both the demand—how many people want to see them—and the supply—how many people want to act in them. My impression is that this supply component, the eagerness of the English to take part in drama, helps explain the larger number of shows. This thought came to mind when I attended a performance of *Ruddigore*, one of Gilbert and Sullivan's lesser-known operettas. It was a Fringe production, and I had to take the Tube to the suburb of Turnham Green to see it. The performance very much reminded me of the Oxford play, with young actors expertly and enthusiastically step-ping into their parts. In commercial terms, it also resembled the Oxford play. Ticket sales—there were just 80 of us crammed into a makeshift theater that felt like a phone booth—seemed hardly suf-ficient to cover the rent, taxes, and electricity bill. There could not have been much left over for the actors and management, so you couldn't say this enterprise represented any kind of good living for the actors.

As I walked out of the Tabard Theatre that June evening, I had the distinct feeling that I had seen an application of Wil-liam Morris's theory about the inherent appeal of labor. Yes, in theater production, some money changes hands, but the explana-tion for why England has such a plethora of shows traces to the supply side: In this country, there are many more people who enjoy the work.

6

The Sporting Life

On leaving Oxford heading south, I found myself paddling into the bosom of one of England's most popular sports . . . rowing.

Downriver from the city, the Thames is swelled by the waters of several tributaries, including the Evenlode and the Cherwell. The river grows to a width of about 75 yards, wide enough to accommodate racing shells of one, two, four, six, and eight rowers (yes, sixes are rare, but I did see one). The wider water is certainly needed, for though the racing shells themselves are narrow slivers of fiberglass, their massive oars reach out some 12 feet on each side, producing an impediment to navigation three times as wide as a powerboat. Furthermore, the rowers are not facing in the direction they are going, so, except for eight-oared boats controlled by a coxswain, they are cruising blind. From time to time, the occupants of a shell turn their heads to check their course, but it's mostly the job of other marine traffic to avoid them. Because the razor-sharp bows of the rowing shells are moving twice as fast as powerboats (10 mph compared to 5 mph), I had to be alert whenever one was near.

On the morning I left Oxford, the river below the town was teeming with shells out for morning practice. Here the Thames is lined with dozens of boathouses belonging to the different Oxford colleges. Peek inside one of these structures and you will see each crammed with racing shells stacked to the ceiling—more, it seems, than human beings could ever have a legitimate need for, as though a product of some insidious, unstoppable arms race.

At one of the college boathouses, a crew of eight young men was disembarking after a workout, and I paddled over to chat with them. They reported that rowing is the most popular sport on campus. "If you're at Oxford any length of time," one boy said, "you'll have been involved in rowing one way or another." Their crew worked out for an hour and a half each morning, which seemed like a lot, but they said it was nothing compared to the three-plus hours of training for the men selected to represent Oxford in the Oxford–Cambridge race.

"Rowing is about all they do," said one, who pointed out that they tend to take easy majors to be able to spare the time—just as college football players in the United States.

"They develop an enormous build. Just mountains of muscle."

As I pushed away from the dock, I asked one last question: "By the way, which college are you?"

"Jesus!" they said all together, rather emphatically.

"Now, now boys, don't swear," I teased, and they laughed. Jesus is the name of one of Oxford's 38 colleges. When founded in 1571, guess what subject the college specialized in.

In the old days, rowing was a man's sport, but not any longer. As I progressed down the river, I saw almost as many female crews as male. However, a puzzling pattern occurs in the choice of coxswains for the male and female boat crews. The cox steers the boat and does all the talking, calling the stroke and motivating the crew with yells of encouragement. In the old days, the cox used a megaphone; today, everyone uses a headset mike and speaker. The requirements for being a cox include light body weight and an aura of congenial authority. On the boats rowed by males, the coxswains are about half male and half female, a nice gender equality that would please the statistically minded. For the female crews, however, the coxes are almost always males, even though males tend to be heavier on average. It is something of a mystery that, in this highly emancipated age, women rowers like the idea of having a male in charge.

Rowing is more than a sport on the Thames; it's a complex part of the economic and social structure. For example, manufacturing and repairing the shells is a significant industry. Great care must be taken in their production to make them especially light and perfectly true. As a result, the boats are astonishingly expensive: several thousand pounds for a budget model and five times that for an elite competition model. Then there is coaching. Many times a day, I saw crews or singles out practicing under the tutelage of a coach. Sometimes the coaches followed the boats by riding a bicycle on the footpath beside the river, but usually he or she tagged along in a special small watercraft steered with handlebars, like a motorcycle. Though these craft might resemble the personal Jet Ski-type water scooters in the States, they are far more sedate. Nowhere on the Thames did I ever see those personal watercrafts that tear the surface and rupture the sound barrier on so many American lakes. The entire Thames is a no-wake zone with a 5 mph speed limit, so a Jet Ski would have no scope on its waters.

Wherever there is sport, there is competition, and the Thames has a long tradition of rowing races. In 1715, a philanthropist, Thomas Doggett, established a race for the Watermen of London, the men who worked the water taxis in the days when the Thames had few bridges. The race is still held today, under the auspices of the Worshipful Company of Fishmongers. Instead of competing in clunky passenger wherries as in the old days, today's contestants row in slim, modern racing sculls. This race probably qualifies as the oldest rowing competition still being held in the world.

Everyone knows about the Oxford–Cambridge race, first rowed in 1829. Now, with live television coverage, the whole country comes to a standstill for 20 minutes while the 4.2-mile contest is waged. Rather perversely, it seems, race organizers have chosen to hold this event on the tidal stretch of the Thames, going upstream from Putney to Mortlake, in the western suburbs of London. This means they have to adjust the start time to match the flood of the incoming tide. Another difficulty with this route on the lower Thames is the wave action in windy conditions. Racing shells are shallow and unseaworthy, and easily swamped: Six boats have sunk in the history of the race, most recently the Cambridge shell in 1978. It doesn't help that the organizers—perverse to a fault—insist the race be held in bitter, blustery March.

The best place to hold rowing races on the Thames is the town of Henley, because of the straight, wide stretch of water there. The people who are clever enough to realize this have also figured out that the best time to do it is in late June when the warm sun is kind to spectators, and the long days allow for many races. When I paddled into Henley at the end of May, they were already erecting, on the right-hand side of the river, the pavilions that would hold the many crews competing in the Henley Royal Regatta. Just a few yards from these pavilions stands the stately building of the Leander Club, which houses the oldest rowing club in the world, founded in 1818.

Henley's week-long festival of boat racing dates back to 1839, and has grown to become the major world rowing competition, with hundreds of competing crews from around the world. The regatta is an extremely complex competition with 19 separate events, including the Grand Challenge Cup, the Stewards' Challenge Cup, the Queen Mother Challenge Cup, and so on. Because the winner in each category is decided by a head-to-head elimination, many hundreds of races must be run. To squeeze them all in on only one course, they start one set of contestants before the pair ahead has finished their race (which typically lasts about six minutes).

I found it difficult enough to get an accommodation in Henley at the end of May. I shuddered to think of the crush that must take place as both rowers and spectators descend on the town during the regatta. Lately, the race has become a social event and tourist highlight. Big companies establish hospitality suites in tents along the course, commercial firms rent houseboats that crowd the river, and thousands wangle entries into the stewards' enclosure. As one can imagine, these multitudes of spectators are not intently watching the rowers hour after hour. They are mainly attending to one another—usually while holding a glass in one hand. The excessive party atmosphere of modern times led one wit to comment that if they banned rowing, Henley would continue unaffected, but if they placed a ban on alcohol, the regatta would collapse immediately.

On leaving Henley after a two-day stay, I saw no partying to distract me as I paddled along the white markers of the 1.3-mile course (heading downriver, but up the course). The banks were silent and empty, occupied only by the occasional stroller on the footpath walking alongside cows munching quietly on green grass. When I reached the end of the course, I saw, standing on an island past the cow pasture . . . an ancient-looking temple! This made me smile: to think that anyone would go to the trouble of erecting an ornamented white marble temple out in the middle of nowhere, not for the worship of anything, but just to be quirky. I had stumbled upon what the English call a "folly," a structure that has no purpose except to bemuse observers. Architectural follies are found in other countries, but they are especially numerous in Britain, the products of a long tradition of whimsy. This particular temple, sheltering the graceful statue of a nymph, was built in 1771, over a half century before the ancient Henley Regatta began.

This matter of rowing raises the larger topic of the place of sport in England. In game after game, one finds that the English have played a pivotal role in developing the sport, or at least an early version of it. Most people know that American football, for example, grew out of rugby. It is less well known that American baseball was adapted from English rounders. This game has a slightly suspect provenance, as I learned when I asked my classmates at Highgate, the London school I attended, if we could put together a game of rounders. I wanted to return home claiming to have played the grandfather of baseball. They didn't say anything at the time, but I detected a certain hesitation. Later my roommate explained the problem: "Jim, rounders is a game for girls!" And it is, in fact, rather tame. Like baseball, rounders uses four bases and the players hit a pitched ball, but the short, flat bat is held in one hand, and one doesn't have much power or control. The girls I saw playing it seemed to assume that the batter's job was merely to put the ball in play; the game had a desultory feel, as if nothing about it really mattered. It was the American addition of the larger, two-handed bat that produced a game the world could take seriously.

Another common feature in the myriad games the English have invented is their quirkiness; they are games that are unusual, even silly, at least at first glance. Cricket is one example. The key to it, the center of attention, is what happens to two tiny pieces of wood that have been balanced on top of three wooden posts behind the batsman. The pitcher (bowler) tries to knock off the pieces of wood, while the batsman guards the wicket, trying to protect them. Among other bizarre features, a cricket game can last for days.

Croquet is another game the English developed that involves special equipment (clunky mallets and wooden balls, nine wire hoops, and two posts) and curious rules—just the kind of game it would be natural to play in the zany world Lewis Carroll created in *Alice in Wonderland*. Darts is another quirky English game, one in which winning requires that you make your score total 501 exactly, not more. To accomplish this, you must hit your needed double score spot, which is a target smaller than the bull's-eye. If you miss and hit some different number that takes your score past 501, your score goes back to zero and you have to start all over again. Hence, for beginners, a game of English darts can last as long as a cricket match.

During my school days in Highgate, I discovered another of these unusual sports. Across the street from my dormitory was a set of courts for a game called Eton Fives. In basic outlines, this is a game of handball with a front wall and two side walls. The walls, however, are very unusual, having ledges that jut out, and a buttress-like structure on the left side. To add a final crazy touch, the floor takes a step down in the middle of the court. The result of all these irregular surfaces is that the ball can bounce unpredictably.

The boys told me this court was modeled after the side of the chapel at Eton, the famous boys' school, where the game was invented. I never quite believed that explanation, however, and I made it one objective of my kayak trip to see this chapel when I arrived in Eton—which lies right on the Thames, across from the city of Windsor.

On my second morning in the area, I went with Carlo, an English kayaker who had befriended me, to the campus of Eton College. We eventually found the central quadrangle where the chapel stands, and persuaded the porter to let us in to see it. Sure enough, there was the Fives court, looking almost exactly like the one I had played on in London—ledges, buttress, and all. The "court" stood alongside the steps of the side entrance to the chapel. The porter said that the boys used that stairway to enter the chapel for the many services they were required to attend back in the 19th century when the game was invented. When they arrived early, they killed time by playing Fives in the nook at the base of the steps.

One can understand that some boys might play an informal handball game against an irregular church wall; there's nothing unusual about that. What is striking and surprising is that other people would take this primitive activity and develop it into a formal game played by large numbers of people. At Eton, the first move to make Fives a sport took place in 1840, when the headmaster had four courts specially built to resemble the original one at the chapel. Today, there are hundreds of Fives courts in Britain, and dozens in other countries, from Switzerland to Nigeria. A national Eton Fives Association promulgates the rules and court requirements, and publicizes dozens of yearly tournaments.

This has been the pattern for sport after sport. In most cases, you can't say that the English *invented* the sport. What they did was take a primitive activity and focus it into a formal, competitive game. The game of badminton illustrates this development. The idea of hitting a shuttlecock with a racket dates back thousands of years. As an aimless pastime, this activity seems to have been pursued in many parts of the world, from Greece to Thailand. What English soldiers in India did back in the late 18th century was take the shuttlecock game and *set up a net*. Now you could clearly miss a shot, so a successful action was clearly distinguished from an unsuccessful one. Thus, a competitive *sport* was born.

To fully develop a sport, however, it's not enough to have a competitive game. You have to have lots of people willing and eager to play it; it is here, I believe, where the English excelled. Inventing a sport means getting the game widely played, widely talked about, widely accepted. Tennis, for example, didn't begin in England (it apparently began in France). But it was the English who first took it up in great numbers, and first established public competitions. We think of England as having started tennis not because of the person who first hit a tennis ball, but because of Wimbledon, where the first tournament was held in 1877.

How do we explain the early English eagerness for developing competitive sports? One wonders if perhaps the trait that lies behind it is the same one that leads the English to embrace the stage. In many respects, participating in a competitive sport is similar to acting in a play. One steps on a stage where others are watching. There is great potential for embarrassment, for looking foolish, for making mistakes. Furthermore, a competitive sport is an activity where someone is bound to lose, and to some extent lose face.

The potential for embarrassment would be especially great in the early days of a game before it becomes familiar and widely recognized. You are being asked to pick up strange implements and manipulate them in a new, artificial way, and you can't say as a way of protective social coloration, "Everyone's doing it."

Imagine that we are back in 1873, at the Duke of Beaufort's manor house in Gloucestershire (near the source of the Thames, as it happens), and two teenage girls are speaking:

> *Naomi:* Cecily, come out and play with me!
> *Cecily:* What's that you have in your hand?
> *Naomi:* It's a new sport we heard the soldiers are playing in India! You use these little racquety things. See? (*Waving racquet back and forth*)
> *Cecily:* It looks quite weird to me.
> *Naomi:* It's loads of fun! You hit these bitsy feather things with it. See? (*Naomi darts to and fro, throwing the shuttlecock in the air, swinging at it, most times missing it. Her bonnet falls off in the process.*) These feather things have to go over that net; otherwise you lose the point. Come and try it!
> *Cecily:* It looks pretty silly to me. How do you know you won't fall and get mud on your party chiffon? (*She pauses, then giggles.*) When the people sipping tea on the veranda see us playing that, they'll think we've gone mad!

If Cecily is French, or Japanese, or Lithuanian, she will probably stay on the porch along with her friends, not risking social opprobrium, and the new sport will remain undeveloped. But because she is English, gifted with that same fine social confidence that may some day propel her eagerly onto the stage, she is willing to take a chance of looking foolish. She strides out upon the grass and joins her friend Naomi, and a sport is born . . . named after the Duke of Beaufort's estate, Badminton.

7
Crooked Everything

The moment of revelation came in Pangbourne, at 7:30 in the evening at The George Hotel. I had ended up there after several hours of anxiety, toiling first to find a safe-enough place to moor my kayak (I settled on leaving it tucked against the bank in the parkland below the town), and then having been turned down for lodging at two B&Bs on opposite sides of town. In spite of the high cost of The George and its location next to the busy railway line, I was grateful to have found a place to sleep. After unpacking, I was heading out the door of my room to get supper when I realized I hadn't the slightest idea how to get to the lobby and the street! I had been led to my room by the cheerful son of the Pakistani owner and had followed him blindly, not thinking to spread a trail of bread crumbs as I went. All I knew was that I had covered an enormous number of twists and turns, and many different steps up and down to my room in this small, two-story building.

As I stood at the door, it dawned on me that my confusion was not an accident. All the buildings I had stayed in since arriving in England had exhibited this complex character, with extra twists and puzzling deflections from a straight and logical passage. I saw that, like the falling apple that hit Isaac Newton on the noggin, the rabbit warren of steps and passageways in The George reflected a larger principle at work in the land. The complexity of this building was a finding that cried out for documentation. I went back into my room, Number 39, dug out my little digital recorder, and, exploring my way back to the lobby, began a moment-by-moment narration of each stairway, doorway, and turn. I've just finished replaying that recording and I am struck by the tone of delight and amazement in my voice as I take note of each new kink in the route.

Before retracing that route, let's compare my results with what they would be in an American lodging. If you were on the second floor of a Holiday Inn in California, to reach the lobby you would make one turn from your door, walk along a hall, go down one or two flights of steps, and push through a door. Perhaps you might encounter an additional turn in the route or an additional door. Basically, you would have a total "crookedness score" of 3 to 5, adding all the turns, doorways, and sets of stairs together.

At The George in Pangbourne, my route back to the lobby required 7 turns, 7 sets of stairs (most just one or two steps at each "flight"), and 4 doorways, for a crookedness score of 18. This raw number, high as it is, doesn't do justice to the complexity of the structure. The crookedness score doesn't reveal that the passageways had irregular walls; the sides angled out and jutted in, so that one point in the hall would be 9 feet wide, and 4 feet wide a few steps later. The ceilings, too, were irregular: low, then higher, then very low. The crookedness score doesn't include the robust squeaking made by the floorboards as I walked along (which was captured by my recorder). In short, the place was a Mother Hubbard's cottage—what Americans would come up with if they built a fairy tale theme park for the delight of little children.

It isn't just the buildings that have this complex quality. The penchant toward the irregular is found in many other artifacts. The George at Pangbourne is, like Newton's falling apple, a singular expression of a universal force at work in English life.

When I first noticed this quaintness as a boy living in England, I was given practical explanations for it. The irregularities found in English artifacts were said to be the product of (1) the ancientness of the country, (2) the lack of resources, and (3) the lack of space. These factors will, to some extent, explain crookedness, as we can illustrate in the case of The George. It is a very old building, as its Tudor facing attests, and it has been modified and remodeled countless times over the generations. Imagine, for example, the havoc wrought by adding an en suite bathroom to each of the 23 rooms. The contractor would have had to chop at walls and floors to run all those pipes, leaving numerous lumps and crevices in the process.

Making alterations might not result in too much irregularity if the owners who made them took a spare-no-expense approach. If they were willing to tear everything out and start over, for example, they could insist on straight halls and level floors. But such radical remodeling costs money—often more than building from scratch. Until very recently, England has been a poor country, and property owners could not afford streamlined alterations. If in, say, 1830, the owner of The George wanted to divide an upstairs hall into four separate bedrooms, he would instruct the carpenters to make the minimal changes to accomplish this. He would not be willing to pay for false walls to cover up the irregularities left by the remodel.

Finally, because England is a small, densely populated country, space for buildings (and within buildings) has been at a premium. This creates a pressure to cram things in. For example, in most English homes, the stairways to the second floor switch direction on the way up, a space-saving feature (the most space-saving stairway is a spiral). In the United States, with more land

and more spacious houses, stairways are more likely to go straight up, without turns.

Let us for a moment set aside Pangbourne's George Hotel, and turn to another area where the theme of crookedness dominates: England's streets and roads. One of the first things an American visitor notices about England is that the streets are not laid out in any geometric pattern. In the United States, the common unit of distance in a town or city is the block. In England, the word *block* has no meaning, so asking a native how many blocks to the railroad station is about as meaningful as asking for the distance in cubits. The grid pattern that an American instinctively relies upon to find his way about towns and cities is unknown, and an American who strides out into the streets quickly becomes disoriented. (When in the middle of such confusions myself, I have often wondered if England has a missing persons list of Yanks who left their hotels for a walk around the block and were never heard from again.)

To get around in England, I used one of three strategies. In small towns like Lechlade or Cricklade, I would simply meander. When a place has fewer than 30 streets, one can follow a process of trial and error to reach any destination. In smaller cities, like Oxford and Guildford, I found the best method was to ask people for directions, get lost after a few hundred feet, then ask again. In a big city where most people on the streets are tourists and haven't a clue—namely London—my only solution was to follow a street map step by step, being careful not to leave my head buried in the map while trying to cross a street.

To explain the irregular character of English streets, one can point to the same basic factors affecting buildings: antiquity, poverty, and space. England's roads and streets arose organically, with footpaths following game trails, and roads superimposed on footpaths. Thus, you could say that English roads were designed by deer and badgers—and are therefore understandably unstraight.

Furthermore, to fix these irregularities would cost a lot of money. To put a straight, wide boulevard through London would cost millions of pounds per foot. So money is a limiting factor. And so is space. To have a London with wide streets would mean eliminating houses, forcing thousands of Londoners to huddle in a tent city in Trafalgar Square.

For many years, I accepted these explanations—antiquity of the country, money, and space—to account for twisted English roads. Then one day back in 1992, while hiking in the Cotswolds (I was searching for the source of the Thames, as it happens), I came across a flat stretch of land where a crew was improving a rural road: bulldozing, grading, and spreading gravel. This road happened to make an "S" turn in the middle of open land, and there was no apparent reason for it. There were no trees, buildings, or creeks for the road to curve around. What was amazing, to my American eye, was that the rebuilders were not making any effort to eliminate or even reduce the "S" turn. It was not a question of money. They were already rebuilding the road, trucking in gravel, bulldozing dirt, and so forth, so they could have easily eliminated the curve. That was when I began to suspect that something more than practical considerations were at work. Perhaps crookedness was an ingrained English trait.

Later in the hike, I came upon a straight-as-an-arrow stretch of road going into Cirencester. At first it seemed that my budding theory of crookedness was being contradicted. The English were able to make straight roads after all. However, a look at the Ordinance Survey map showed that this road was the exception that proved the rule. This straight road, the A433, was identified as a Roman road called the Fosse Way! This suggests you can't use antiquity as the complete explanation for crooked roads: The Romans were able to build straight roads in AD 400.

Some years later, on a hike across Yorkshire, I came upon another straight stretch of road running down the side of a mountain. It was a gravel side road, not used by traffic—more of a track than a road—but I could sight along it straight as a string. I was getting to know England well enough to be able to make a prediction: *I'll bet this is a Roman road!* Sure enough, the Ordinance Survey map confirmed that it was.

That, after 2,000 years, the only straight roads in the country are the ones built by foreigners is strong evidence for a cultural force deep at work in the land. Badgers didn't design English roads; Englishmen did.

In seeking to understand the cultural trait that underlies crookedness, let us shift our attention to another artifact: the English bathroom sink—specifically the location of the hot and cold water taps. Tourists who stay only in modern luxury hotels are unaware of this issue, because the practice of putting the hot water on the left is generally followed in modern commercial buildings. But visitors who stray to older apartments, farmhouses, and thatched cottages will discover something hilarious going on with the taps, for you never know which side the hot water is on! There is a tendency for the hot water to come out the left tap—but this is only a tendency, nothing you could bet on. This irregular result, I believe, traces to the same impulse that leads to crooked roads and buildings.

How should we describe this trait? English writer George Orwell explained it by declaring that "the English are not intellectual. They have a horror of abstract thought, they feel no need for any philosophy or systematic 'world view.'" I think it's going too far to say the English are not intellectual, for the country produces plenty of brainy people, in both the arts and the sciences. What seems to be lacking, especially among the average, nontechnical populace, is a disposition toward general principles. Perhaps one could say that the English tend to be *atheoretical*: They don't naturally seek out an overarching principle to tie things together.

Consider how this disinclination toward theory might play out in streets and roads. You don't need to have studied Euclid to grasp the idea that a straight line is the shortest distance between two points. A theoretically minded person would incorporate this rule into the building and rebuilding of roads, so that new roads would tend to be straight—and old roads would tend to be straightened over time. If you're atheoretical, this point doesn't occur to you, or doesn't weigh very strongly, and roads stay crooked.

If you're remodeling a hotel, one general principle is to have fewer steps and turns—for reasons of safety and convenience. If you heed this general rule, you will tend to eliminate them in a remodel. If this overall point doesn't weigh in your thinking, then a twisty corridor will seem good enough to get the job done.

If you're installing a sink and you are theoretically minded, your brain reaches out for some general principle to decide which faucet should be hot. One obvious idea would be to follow the established custom, so that everyone automatically knows where to expect the hot water, saving time and vexation. If, on the other hand, you are an atheoretical plumber and you are sitting under a new bathroom sink with a hot water line in your hand, you connect it to the tap that's closest to your nose.

Many commentators have noted the nonlogical streak that seems to crop up in England. The great 19th-century English author Anthony Trollope explored this theme in one of his novels, *The American Senator.* In the story, a senator comes for an extended visit to England and makes a thorough investigation of its institutions. He is appalled by the failure of the country to follow obvious first principles in its social and political life. He found the House of Lords offensive because it flatly contradicts the principle of democratic representation: You gain a seat in this legislative body not by winning an election but by holding a title of nobility. The senator is so vexed by the inconsistencies, and so eager to straighten out the benighted English, that he goes to the trouble of giving a lecture in London at the end of his visit, which he entitles, "The Irrationality of Englishmen." As he delivers his speech at the huge auditorium at St. James's Hall, ticking off one logical contradiction after the other, the audience grows increasingly hostile, until a riot is brewing. To prevent the outbreak of violence, the chief of police intervenes and declares the lecture over. The senator finally makes his way safely back to his hotel and concludes that "the want of reason among Britishers was so great, that no one ought to treat them as wholly responsible beings."

Of course, Trollope exaggerates for dramatic effect, but he does highlight an important theme: We need some way to account for the strange *uncertainty* that infuses English artifacts and practices. Time and again, the visitor bumps up against puzzling irregularities that leave one feeling that the country has been constructed by forest sprites. My final example takes the form of a question: If you are driving a boat down the Thames, which side of the river should you take when approaching an oncoming boat?

When this question first arose for me, facing an oncoming narrowboat, here's how I analyzed the problem: I knew that in England they drive on the left side of the road, so I reasoned that they would apply this general principle to river traffic. Therefore, I paddled to the left side, quite proud of myself for transcending my own cultural bias. Well, the narrowboat headed toward me. I veered farther to the left, hugging the bank. At the last moment, the oncoming boat changed course to avoid me, but I could tell from the scowl on the driver's face that he was irritated, and thought me rude and unknowledgeable. At the next lock, I asked the lockkeeper about the principle. With a smile, realizing that he was making a point that would seem contradictory, he said that the rule on the Thames is to stay to the *right*. "Just like in America. It should be easy for you," he said with a wink.

You see what I mean?! Maybe my theory about the English being atheoretical is misguided, but something strange is going on, and the traveler needs to be prepared for it.

Some weeks after finishing my trip, I visited a website that recorded travelers' comments about lodgings in Britain, and I looked up what they were saying about The George Hotel in

Pangbourne. One woman, who was English, wrote that she was generally pleased with the hotel, but reported being mystified with the plumbing:

> The bathroom had bath and shower, but over 3 nights we never did figure out how to get the water out of the bath taps!! That being said, I ran my bath through the shower. . . .

Welcome to England, my dear!

8
Tradition

For my ninth night on the river, just below Abingdon, I had high hopes for a suitable camping site at Little Wittenham Wood, a nature preserve managed by the Northmoor Trust. The Ordinance Survey map showed the preserve as an inch of green-shaded area along the river, meaning it was free of houses and farms, thereby free of human beings who might disturb my rest.

It was after 7 p.m. when I let myself through Day's Lock and cruised quietly over to the wild land on the right-hand side of the river. The land was thickly lined with overhanging branches, but I managed to find a gap beneath the limbs and slid my boat up to the bank. I then began to understand that land untouched by the human hand is land where nature runs riot. England is a damp, cool country where anything made of chlorophyll thrives and, if left untouched, thrives still more. I climbed up onto the bank, pushing aside weeds and bushes, hoping to discern a possible open spot beyond the edge of the river. I didn't take many steps, however, because the vegetative barrier consisted of the head-high bowers of stinging nettle that grow so profusely in this damp, cool country. Although I can stand, and occasionally enjoy, the brief frisson of a nettle's sting, it was impossible to contemplate sleeping in it. It would be like trying to camp among bee hives. I was forced to conclude that a nature preserve, if not red, then green "in tooth and claw," was not a hospitable place for human flesh.

On the opposite side of the river stood a newly mowed hay field dotted with large, half-ton rolled bales. It seemed a better option for sleeping than battling the jungle of nettle, but it lacked privacy; a footpath ran along the edge by the river. I asked a woman who was meandering along the path with field glasses for bird watching if she thought it would be all right for a person to sleep in the field. She said she didn't see why not, and then eyed me with a mixture of pity and anxiety, not sure what to expect from a man who slept in fields.

I waited for darkness to gather and for the dog walkers to go home for the evening, and then made my bed up against the side of one of the bales. On this night, I developed a camping innovation to combat the cold that can so easily penetrate my lightweight sleeping bag. On the field, scattered here and there, were swatches of dried hay left by the bailer. I raked this up with my fingers and piled the loose hay on my sleeping bag, and then pulled the ground cloth over the top. It made an 8-inch-thick quilt that kept me perfectly warm all night.

The next morning, I loaded my gear and set off down the river. After having had both a lunch and supper of nothing but nuts, raisins, and energy bars the previous day, I was eager to find a restaurant capable of serving me a hearty breakfast. In three miles, I came to the Shillingford Bridge Hotel, an imposing traditional building standing high above the river whose appearance promised superb dining fare. Alas, I had not reckoned with the implacable uniformity of the English breakfast.

One key to a good restaurant is variety in the dishes being offered, under the reasonable theory that patrons don't like to eat the same old thing day after day. As concerns lunch and dinner, England seems finally to have mastered this idea—probably because foreigners have largely taken over the establishments that serve those meals. However, breakfast is still largely in the hands of Englishmen, whose premise when it comes to cuisine appears to be, "if it ain't broke, don't fix it." Under this rule, all lodgings in England offer exactly the same breakfast fare. There will be a sideboard of dry cereals, a pitcher of orange juice from concentrate, toast, containers of yogurt, some fruit, and coffee and tea. Occasionally, you will find a few other items, like kipper— a smelly, bony smoked fish said to be edible—and oatmeal, but these hardly count as alternatives. If this fare is not sufficient for your needs, you will be offered, with a little drum roll of pride, the full cooked English breakfast: eggs, sausage, bacon, tomatoes, and baked beans.

Now from one point of view, the B&B hostess is right to take pride in her full cooked English breakfast, because there's a lot of food and calories there, and on these grounds no one has any right to complain. The trouble is that this dish is exactly the same, day after day, hotel after hotel, from one end of England to the other. There seems to be no sensitivity to the plight of a human being who might desire another option. I found this limitation difficult to understand. In my little hometown of Sandpoint, Idaho, the restaurants have a dozen different well-known breakfast entrees, and vie with one another by inventing additional creations, from orange pecan French toast to an item at the Blue Moon Café called "the howler." It was this cornucopia of variety that I unconsciously anticipated when I crawled out from under that hay bale, and which I fully expected the stately Shillingford Bridge Hotel to offer.

The head waiter led me across the plushly carpeted dining room and seated me at a table with a starched white linen tablecloth, thick linen napkins, and hefty, gleaming silverware. A bus-boy filled my glass with ice water, and the waitress hurried up to me with a pleasant smile.

"Would you like the buffet?" she asked, indicating the side-board with the cold cereals and yogurt cups. "Or, if you like," she continued, "I could serve you a full cooked English breakfast."

You could practically hear my high appetite hopes hit the carpet with a thud, but I made an effort to hide my disappointment. After all, she could not be held responsible for the bland culinary willfulness of an entire nation. "Do you have anything else?" I asked gently. "Like . . . do you have an omelet?"

She shook her head.

"Do you know what an omelet is?" I was not being catty in asking this question. It had suddenly occurred to me that one explanation for the relentless monotony of the food was that no one knew of any other possibilities. For a moment, I fell into the mind-set of Trollope's American senator, thinking that I might be able to rescue the English breakfast by instructing the people of the country about the existence of other options.

Yes, she said, she knew what an omelet was, but the hotel didn't have them.

"What about French toast?" She shook her head: not available. Again, as politely as possible, I asked, "Do you know what that is?" She claimed to know, but I didn't entirely believe her.

"What about pancakes? Have you heard of them?" Yes, yes, she claimed to know all about them, but the hotel didn't have them, either.

"Or waffles?" An edge of irritation was creeping into my voice. I was beginning to see my theory of abysmal ignorance was not, after all, the explanation for the breakfast boredom. The English do know that other breakfast entrees are available—they must know, for goodness sakes. They visit other countries. France with its French toast is only 20 miles across the English Channel.

I began to understand that what I was probably experiencing here is the well-known English commitment to tradition. This certainly is a character streak that runs through English culture. And it has many positive benefits. It's what sustains the British monarchy, and the House of Lords, and the swan upping, and the Worshipful Company of Fishmongers, and a thousand other English institutions that give the country so much of its charm. It's perhaps forgivable if this same trait shows up in a rather plodding John Bull stubbornness from time to time.

"So, would you prefer the cooked breakfast?" the waitress prodded.

"Yes, that would be fine," I said with an understanding smile. After all, it would at least be nourishing. And who was I to be so finicky? If the English had the fortitude to bear up against German bombing day after day in the blitz, surely I could endure the full cooked English breakfast, day after day.

Tradition may account for majestic institutions like the British monarchy, and for nationwide bothers like the full cooked English breakfast, but it also accounts for some almost unnoticeable tics as well. The one I'm thinking of is the resolute refusal to provide hotel guests with facecloths, or washcloths as we call them.

I noticed this lack on my first night on this journey, at the Red Lion Inn in Cricklade. This was a four-star establishment whose bathroom offered many deluxe features, including a heated towel rack and a wide assortment of free soaps, shampoos, and lotions. It also had an abundance of different sizes of thick, fluffy towels, but with all this linen came not a single facecloth. I found this surprising because in America, every lodging house, down to the very meanest, provides this item. In England, on the other hand, as the case of the Red Lion foreshadowed, facecloths are almost never provided, whether the establishment is two-star, three-star, or four-star. (I've never been able to afford five-star lodging, so I'll leave it to better-heeled readers to complete the research on this point.)

How do we account for the absence of the facecloth? One possibility is that it simply isn't needed: It is an American frill that the practical English have sensibly gone without. But it *is* needed. Try washing off any actual spot of dirt from your body—say a grease spot—without it. It seems especially true that women would need it to remove makeup. This thought aroused my curiosity about how English women got along without a facecloth, and I undertook to explore the issue: "How do you remove your makeup without a facecloth?" was my survey question. The first woman I asked replied, with some asperity, that she didn't use makeup, so she couldn't answer my question. That exchange alerted me to the fact that my research was a rather delicate enterprise, whose purpose might easily be misunderstood. If the woman didn't use makeup, then my question might rather insult her; if she did, then the question might implicitly accuse her of overdoing it. It was not a query to make of strangers.

I laid the problem aside for several days until I found myself in a conversation where sufficient rapport had been built up to allow me to ask my question without giving offense. My respondent was with a group in a pub celebrating one of life's small triumphs and she had a gay, devil-may-care attitude. She was not the least put off by my question.

"Oh, I dampen the edge of a towel to rub it off."

"So that means you end up with a soiled and partly wet towel?" I asked.

"Well, I suppose that's true."

"Doesn't that bother you?"

She reflected a moment. "I suppose it's not ideal. But one manages."

I felt very pleased, for her report clearly documented that English-speaking peoples need facecloths. That left me with the idea that, in England, facecloths simply hadn't been discovered, and there was fame and gratitude to be earned by pointing out this fact in a letter to the *Times.* This hope prevailed until it was knocked into a cocked hat by my stay at Sue Simmons's B&B in Marlow.

I have changed the names of most other people in this account, but in the case of Sue Simmons, I have made an exception, for she deserves notoriety as the doyenne of the most perfect B&B in England. The only disadvantage of her establishment, from my point of view, was that it stood at the end of a two-mile walk up a long hill high above town, and the crazy street numbering (forest sprites again) had me walking past it and knocking on the wrong door. But once I was inside her walls, I knew I was in the presence of the J. S. Bach of B&Bs. The place was flawlessly decorated and spotlessly clean, and each room had everything a traveler could want, whether it be a hair dryer, or a jar of cotton swabs and cotton balls for removing makeup. On the nightstand was a clock radio with alarm, actually displaying the correct time (not always the case in other B&Bs).

All this was very pleasing, but the crowning glory was the linen supply. Along with the different sizes of fluffy white towels was a perfectly wonderful, proper *washcloth!* I gave a little cry of surprise and delight.

Then I realized that this little square of cotton fabric would compel me to change my theory about the absence of washcloths. They were *not* unknown in this land. Some prior explorer must have come before me and spread the message of their useful necessity.

After unpacking, I went downstairs to chat with Sue, a slim, youngish woman with short, light brown hair, and an earnest, attentive air: She was the kind of woman you'd want in charge of your blood transfusion. I soon brought the conversation around to my discovery.

"I noticed you give the guests washcloths along with the towels . . . ?"

"Oh yes, of course. Flannels we call them. It's on the list of requirements."

Now I was amazed. "Requirements . . . ?"

"Of the English Tourist Board. They have a long list of everything a B&B ought to have. When the inspector comes, he checks off each one. It affects your rating," she said, nodding gravely. Sue was wide-eyed and almost reverent as she described the ordeal of this inspection. Just as in Gogol's *The Government Inspector,* the Tourist Board inspector comes incognito, pretending to be an ordinary guest. On the morning after, he reveals his true identity, and then, in a critique lasting several hours, he goes over the establishment's shortcomings. Sue was frustrated because no matter how many of the smaller requirements she met—like giving guests flannels—her B&B could never get more than two stars since her rooms lacked the major requirement of an en suite bathroom.

I found this all very interesting, but I was forced to admit that it shoved my theories about the lack of facecloths in England into the dustbin of history. At supper in the pub across the wheat fields from Sue's house, I pondered the conundrum: washcloths are useful, the English know they're useful, even their government knows they're useful and requires them. Nevertheless, they don't appear in hotels and B&Bs. Why not?

After grappling with this puzzle for some time, I was driven by a process of elimination to the conclusion that the explanation was tradition, the same force that confines breakfast entrees to the full cooked English breakfast. At some early time in the nation's pre-history—the reign of King John, or King Arthur, or King Canute—nobody had any facecloths. Perhaps they didn't care about dirty faces back then, or perhaps all they had was fox skins and bear pelts to work with, and these weren't suitable. So it became traditional not to have facecloths, and this custom has been doggedly upheld, century after century, dynasty after dynasty, overpowering arguments of convenience, of common sense, and even the mandates of bureaucracies.

If someone has a better explanation, I'd love to hear it.

The next morning, after a fine sleep, I came down to the sun-lit breakfast table, and greeted Sue as she came out of the kitchen. She enquired about my visit to the pub the night before; I reported that her recommendation was excellent, and that her directions about taking the footpaths to reach it had been flawless.

"What would you like for breakfast?" she asked gaily.

The question had an open-ended quality. It did not foreshadow the fatalistic choice between the sideboard or the full cooked English breakfast. Her inflection suggested that I really could have anything in the world for breakfast that my heart desired. I broke into a broad grin. *One miracle had already occurred at Sue Simmons's Bed and Breakfast,* I thought, *perhaps there was room for another.*

"Could you make me an omelet?" I asked cautiously.

"Of course."

"You mean, you really . . . actually . . . can do omelets here?" I asked.

"Certainly. What kind would you like? Would you like cheese, or . . . ?"

"Oh, cheese would be fine," I said quickly, not wanting to endanger this second miracle by shaking the wishing tree too hard, asking for a Denver omelet, let's say, or the fisherman's supreme. Sue took my order back to the kitchen and in due course returned with a sizzling cheese omelet on a hot plate.

I'm sure it's not the only omelet that has ever been served for breakfast in England. It's just the only one I tasted.

9
Lesson in Patience

"I wonder if you could help me?"

This was perhaps my most frequently used opening line on my Thames journey, and one that, with one notorious exception, always produced a good result. This particular introduction occurred at the leisure center (fitness club) in Windsor, addressing a middle-aged man seated with two little girls on a couch in the lounge. My kayak had been resting for the past two days on a patch of grass inside the club's employee parking lot, three blocks from the Thames. Now, after visiting Windsor, I wanted to get moving again.

"Watch your little sister while I help this gentleman," the man told the older child, and we went out to the parking lot. I grabbed the handle on the bow, and he took the one on the stern, and together we carried the kayak down the street to the riverside.

In a few minutes, my gear was stowed and I was underway, heading for the Weybridge area. The map showed this as a rather built-up area, for I was moving into the suburbs of London. Even at this morning hour, I was already starting to worry about how I would spend the night. I would not likely find a handy B&B next to the river, and finding a private, secluded camping spot might prove to be difficult. I decided that if I saw a useable patch of forest even as early as 2 p.m., I would stop and make use of it.

The land near Windsor is hilly—a welcome change from the flat bottomland that borders the Thames for most of its length.

Windsor Castle itself stands on a low bluff, and, a few miles away, the Air Forces Memorial occupies another prominence. After 20 minutes of paddling I reached Runnymede, the spot on the Thames where, in 1215, rebellious barons forced King John to sign the famous document known as the Magna Carta.

We Americans, with our profound commitment to legalism, are especially interested in Runnymede. We believe that the progress of mankind is achieved by the approval of paper documents that say in words the nice things that should happen in the world. For example, we venerate our written Constitution, supposing that it is the foundation for the country's success. In the same vein, Americans revere the Magna Carta, supposing it to be the document that first established citizen rights and the rule of law. In this spirit, Americans have turned Runnymede into a shrine. It was an American who—in 1929—donated the Runnymede property for a memorial park, and it was the American Bar Association that has erected a monument there.

The English, however, are a nonlegalistic people. They seem to understand by instinct that culture determines social and political behavior, not words inscribed on paper. The first proof of this spirit of informality is that England does not have a written constitution. The government operates on the basis of common sense and traditions. For example, the timing of elections is not legally specified. It is simply traditional that the prime minister should call for an election within five years of the previous one. There is no official bill of rights protecting freedom of speech or assembly; in England, these freedoms simply are upheld when it comes down to particular cases. With their unconcern for documentary foundations, it is not surprising that the English ignored the mud banks of Runnymede for all those centuries before the Americans took an interest.

In terms of the historical facts, the English skepticism of the Magna Carta would seem fully justified. It was hardly a document establishing modern civil rights, or human rights. It was a treaty-like bargain between rebellious barons and the king, and its main clauses upheld the traditional privileges of the barons. The Magna Carta, one might say, was a document that enshrined *warlord* rights. Subsequent events proved, in any case, that a document alone, when unsupported by cultural and political reality, is mere paper. The Magna Carta remained in force only three months before King John repudiated it and plunged the country into civil war.

Of course, England has plenty of laws—Parliament having been busy for centuries producing them—but the spirit in which they are applied reflects the country's pragmatic attitude toward legal mandates. My wife Judy and I were beneficiaries of this sensible approach when we spent a year in England in 1992. We had failed to obtain a long-term visa before we went, and so we were issued a one-month permit when we went through the Immigration office on arriving. After months of living happily and unmolested in Devon, we took a brief trip to Spain. On returning to England, the Immigration officer frowned when he saw our passports.

"You have only a temporary permit, which is expired," he said. "You're really not supposed to be allowed to enter the country."

"Oh dear," I said. "We're returning to our home in Devon. Isn't there some way . . . ?

"Let me see," said the officer, and he busied himself filling out forms and stamping documents. Finally, he handed back our passports. "There, that should work," he said with a wink.

And it did—as long as we stayed clear of Immigration officers, for the passport stamps allowed only another single month of residence in the country.

Months later, it was time to leave for the States. Judy was terrified that an official at the airport might see our expired visa stamps and take us off to jail.

At the document control station, the official noticed the discrepancy. "Did you know these visas are out of date?"

"Oh really? Oh my goodness! What should we do?"

He gave me a wry smile. "I suppose since you're leaving the country, it really doesn't matter," he said as he handed back the passports and waved us on.

A few miles after leaving Runnymede, I passed under the M25 motorway near Staines, about the tenth highway overpass I'd paddled under on this trip. I always kept these bridges in mind as temporary shelters from possible heavy rain, but I knew this structure would not solve my homelessness problem for the evening. To try to camp in the roaring, echoing envelope of sound beneath a motorway bridge would be like a night spent in Bedlam, complete with screams.

At 4 p.m., still having found no suitable campsite, I reached Penton Hook Lock, tied the kayak to a bollard on the upstream side, and climbed out. The area to the east of the lock consisted of residential housing, but on the west bank was a little island with a grassy area on the upriver point. I inspected the ground there and it seemed relatively free of the goose droppings so often encountered in these riverside spots. It was a little early in the day to stop, but I had the feeling it was the best campsite I was going to find. Although the area teemed with people when I stopped, including cyclists as well as walkers on the Thames path, I reasoned that it would be adequately private after the lockkeeper went home, and the spectators, hikers, and dog walkers retired for the night.

I strongly suspected that camping was not allowed in the area, but no one had explicitly forbidden me to camp. It was my aim to keep it that way by not letting any policeman, lockkeeper, or park official suspect my intentions. I studiously avoided my prized spot, and took up a position on the other side of the lock, so that I could surreptitiously supervise it, pretending to be just a casual day visitor to the lock.

I found ways to kill the many hours before the summer sun of Britain set. One project was to work on memorizing a Shakespeare sonnet. On kayak journeys, I make a practice of bringing along one of these to memorize. For this trip, I was working on Sonnet 116, "Let me not to the marriage of true minds admit impediments." I had it about half committed to memory at this point, which, because it is only a 14-line poem, was a pretty pathetic showing, I agree. Then I took a walk around the tan brick duplexes of the housing development and explored along the road, in the process discovering no restaurants or grocery stores nearby.

I returned to my old position at the lock and prepared to nibble on supper. The mainstays of my kayaking diet in America, peanut butter and energy bars, were both elusive in England. Whereas peanut butter is practically the staff of life in the United States, with store shelves restocked daily with large jars of many brands, it is a rare food in England. If you can find it at all, it tends to be displayed in the specialty foods nook where they put weird, foreign items like pickled grasshoppers from Madagascar.

The peanut butter comes in a tiny jar, about the size of the one containing the grasshoppers and, given its stigmatized status in the store, it has probably been on the shelf for about as long. The upshot is that no American wants to buy peanut butter in England, even if he can find it.

Energy bars—the ones with more than five grams of protein—are also uncommon in England. Typical supermarkets do not carry any—as compared to American stores that have entire sections offering 10 or 15 brands. However, with persistence, I did learn that some Boots pharmacies carry the American Adkins protein bars at the prescription counter, and the organic food store chain Holland and Barrett has several quite satisfactory energy bars. I dined on one of these this particular evening, supplementing my fare with nuts and raisins.

At last, the orange sun pressed against the low hills on the horizon, the lockkeeper disappeared for the day, boat traffic ceased, and the lock area was deserted. I gathered up my backpack, ready to make my move. At just that precise moment, a group of young adults, laughing and chattering, descended into the lock area. They crossed the little footbridge that spans the lock, and, without any hesitation or shyness, they took possession of my camping spot! The three couples seemed to have planned a sunset party, complete with food, wine, and romance (they were already necking). They had brought along blankets and an electric lantern: Even if they had not planned to spend the entire night, they were obviously going to be there for a long, long time.

Their insouciance took my breath away. The utter injustice of it! After I had carefully nurtured and supervised this camping option for hours—now blithely taken away by people who weren't even aware of me and my predicament!

But I had to face facts, and I began mulling other camping options. Adjacent to the lock is a large island, Penton Hook Island, which appears to be parkland, reached by a series of footbridges across the weir. All afternoon, dog walkers and holidaymakers had strolled on the paths around it, but this traffic seemed to have ceased. I put myself through the lock and paddled the kayak around to the island, found a landing place, and unloaded the boat. Though it was after 10 and nearly dark, I waited another half hour to be sure all walkers were gone before spreading my ground cloth at the edge of the footpath. Once in the sleeping bag, I discovered I had not waited long enough. A jogger clopped by on the path next to me, and a little later, a man came walking his dog, which was not on a leash. Fortunately, the dog was friendly and just wanted to lick my face. I had hoped neither visitor would report my presence: I was pretty sure camping wasn't permitted here either.

The night passed, with me awake much of it, as usually happens when I'm camping in a semipublic spot. At 3:30 a.m., the sky started to lighten. I knew I ought to get moving before early morning walkers came, but I was not fast enough to miss the first with his two dogs. I gave him an embarrassed good morning, and he replied in kind. The dogs were not on a leash, but again they were patient and well behaved, and stopped their snuffling of me soon after their master urged them away. (Even dogs are remarkably polite in England, obviously reflecting something about the character of their masters. During the trip, I encountered dogs in several dozen situations and not once did they snarl or bark.)

After the dog walker passed, I quickly slipped out of my sleeping bag, dressed, and packed. Within a few minutes, the boat was loaded, and I was away, gliding triumphantly out onto the water, having conquered another night on the Thames at a cost of zero pounds.

Some days later, at an Internet café, I had an experience that ties into this camping event in a subtle but significant way.

The establishment was supervised by a young Indian man who made espressos and operated the till. The café had twelve computers—five downstairs and seven in an upstairs room at the top of a tiny, winding stairway. I paid him £4 for two hours usage, climbed to the upstairs room, which was empty, picked what I thought was the best of the seven computers, and started pecking away. My objective was to compose a segment of my travel journal for my e-mail correspondents.

This job proved to be especially frustrating because the caps lock key on the keyboard of this machine was where the shift key was located on my computer keyboard back home. I had to keep erasing and retyping whole lines that had been typed in all caps. To add to the confusion, this computer also had a maddening double glitch fouling up the quotation mark key.

The general practice on English computers is for the quotation mark key to be located on the @ key, and they put the @ where the quotation mark key is found on American keyboards. I had been getting used to this reversed location on other computers during the trip, allowing for it with a broad-minded cultural relativism. Who's to say, I kept reminding myself, which country is right, because it's an arbitrary choice at bottom.

Well, on this particular computer, the forest sprites of English crookedness had stepped in to play a diabolical trick: The labels on the keys said one thing—the English pattern—but actually produced *the American result!* So to produce a quotation mark, I had to override what I had learned about English computers and override what the keys on this computer said.

While this computer drove me to distraction mechanically, I was also being tortured intellectually, slow to fashion the words to express the subtle philosophical and emotional points I wished to convey. I composed whole paragraphs and then deleted them, and started again, only to look up and discover I had been typing in caps. I erased again and typed, and erased, and typed. Finally, toward the end of the second hour, I had honed my elusive thoughts into brilliant, precise expression. A message appeared on the screen that I had 10 minutes left and that I must save my work or lose it. This didn't trouble me because I had been keeping track of the time, and had plenty of minutes to spare to complete my task. I put the finishing touches on the document and was just preparing to save and send it when the screen went dead blank. The computer message lied: I did not have 10 minutes left, but only 20 seconds. The English forest sprites had struck again! Frantic clicking of the mouse confirmed that I had forever lost the intricate, perceptive essay I had created in two hours of stressful labor.

But then a surprising thing happened. Yes, for a few seconds I felt fury. But within a minute of experiencing this outrageous injustice, a relaxed mood came upon me. I didn't want to kill anybody; I didn't even want to raise my voice about my loss. I was so mellow that I found myself starting to look on the bright side: The material I just composed could have been flawed, or in poor taste, and would have disgraced me in the eyes of the intended e-mail recipients had it been sent. The computer may have done me a favor by destroying my work. *Everything happens for the best,* I found myself thinking. *The world is wiser than we can possibly know.* I went down the stairs and bid the Indian cashier a cheerful goodbye, not even commenting that his computer just destroyed two hours of work and entirely wasted my £4 in the bargain.

I pushed out the door into the gentle noonday sun, and wondered what accounted for my equanimity. I did not do anything to achieve it. I did not bite my lip, or repeat a mantra, or take a Xanax. The spirit of patience simply blossomed upon me unasked. Then my brain made a connection: It said that what I was feeling lined up with that night at Penton Hook—the cosmic vibrations were the same. That frustrating camping episode at the lock was a training session in learning to accept the improbable disappointments that crop up in this charming country.

10

Enchanting Canal

After leaving Penton Hook, I faced an unusual challenge for a traveler: How to make it take longer to get to my destination. I had set aside 29 days for the entire expedition on the Thames, and, only halfway through my time, I had already reached the outskirts of London. If I didn't do something to slow myself down, I would be at the Thames Barrier—the end of the river by my definition—in just a few more days of paddling. The logical solution to this happy plight was to take a side trip. Inspiration came from the narrowboats I was seeing daily on the Thames. These boats were narrow because they came from, or were going to, the canals that joined the Thames at various points. To use up my extra days, I thought it fitting that I should divert to one of these, and see for myself what canal travel was like.

England has an extensive canal network—more than 110 different canals extending some 1,500 miles. Most of them were developed in the period between 1770 and 1830, when "canal mania" struck the country. In that era, people discovered that bulk goods, especially coal, could be transported much more cheaply on water than by draft animals on the muddy tracks that served as roads. Another advantage of water transportation was its gentleness. The Trent and Mersey Canal, finished in 1771, was funded by the famed potter Josiah Wedgwood, who was fed up with having his delicate plates and urns smashed to bits when jolted around the country on the backs of horses.

By the early 19th century, a canal passed through practically every significant town in the middle of England. They were all linked in an extensive network, with the River Thames as the connecting hub.

The biggest waterway of them all, the Grand Union Canal from London to Birmingham, was 286 miles long with 236 locks. It connected to the Thames at Oxford (via the Oxford Canal) and also at Slough, and ended at Paddington in London, right next to Paddington Station.

With the advent of railroads and improved roads for trucks, the canal system was gradually eclipsed as a mode of commercial transportation. By the mid-20th century, canals were white elephants—of no use to anybody, allowed to silt up or collapse, and sometimes filled in and paved over for highways and shopping centers. Then a remarkable second tide of interest in canals set in—another "canal mania" as it were—a movement to preserve the canals and redirect their function toward tourism and pleasure boating.

The leader of this movement to save the canals was a remarkable English writer and crusader, Tom (L. T. C.) Rolt. Rolt was, like me, a long-distance water traveler, one who took a special interest in culture and customs. In 1939, he and his new bride, Angela, made an extended trip on the canals in central England in a narrowboat, the *Cressy*. He wrote of his adventure in a book that became immensely popular, *Narrow Boat*, first published in 1944. In the book, Rolt extols the pleasures of leisurely, contemplative canal travel, but points out that the old canals were falling into decrepitude. After the war, Rolt was instrumental in founding the Inland Waterways Association, a voluntary group promoting restoration and maintenance of canals.

In many ways, Tom Rolt echoed the values of the social philosopher William Morris. In fact, Rolt and Angela took the *Cressy* up the Thames on what he called a "pilgrimage" to see Kelmscott, Morris's estate at Lechlade.

Both Rolt and Morris deplored large, impersonal organizations, whether commercial or governmental, and set high value on small communities. They also admired craft-type production, and valued old-fashioned farming methods where workers could take pride in cultivating and harvesting food. "The land is not a food factory," said Rolt, "to be exploited by large highly mechanized ranches run by businessmen and mechanics. . . . The land needs husbandmen, not machines and their slaves; it offers a way of life, not a source of profit." Rolt believed the physical world has an underlying harmony, and that man needs to respect this natural order to achieve his own happiness.

Like Morris, Rolt argued against focusing on commercial success: "There are two courses open to each man in his brief lifetime: either he can seek the good life, or he can struggle for wealth and power; the former emphasises spiritual, the latter material values." Rolt urged those who valued the cultural and spiritual values encompassed by the canals to defend them. "If the canals are left to the mercies of economists and scientific planners," he wrote, "before many years are past the last of them will become a weedy, stagnant ditch, and the bright boats will rot at the wharves, to live on only in old men's memories."

Rolt's campaign to save the canals succeeded brilliantly. Today, England has scores of canal trusts and preservation societies working to restore and operate these old waterways. A fleet of some 30,000 narrowboats, in the care of dozens of boat hire firms, gives vacationers the opportunity to put themselves into intimate, leisurely contact with land and nature.

My decision about which canal to take was made quite casually. On my map, I simply poked my finger at the next canal that joined the Thames. Had I studied the options for years, however, I don't think I could have made a more fortunate choice, both in terms of the history enveloping my destination, and the charms of the journey itself.

The canal I chose is known as the Wey Navigation, because it makes use of the River Wey as its water supply. It is a rather short canal, running 16 miles from the town of Weybridge on the Thames to the cathedral city of Guildford. It was built in 1651, over a century before most of England's canals, which makes it practically the oldest in the country. In 1964, its commercial life over, the owners donated it to the National Trust, the venerable environmental charity that manages hundreds of historic and scenic properties across Britain.

The entrance to the canal was rather hard to locate among the various little bays and channels at the mouth of the Wey. I nosed in and out of several places before coming upon it, an imposing double lock system that towered 30 feet above me. I moored the kayak at the dock below and went up the stairways to investigate. In the little lockkeeper's cabin, I found Carrie, the lockkeeper. She explained that the rest of the locks on the canal are unmanned;

I would need to take along a crank handle to open and close the sluices myself. The charge for this herky chunk of steel was £15 (which would be refunded when I returned it the following week). She also sold me a visitor's pass, £4.20 for my kayak for a week. (The Wey Navigation canal is one of the few National Trust properties that covers all its maintenance and operation costs from admission charges.)

I ate a quick breakfast in Weybridge—at a little café run by Italians, where I was able to order a sausage baguette. Then I returned to the lock and let Carrie manage the gates and sluices that lifted me and my kayak up to the beginning of the canal.

It was a Saturday morning, and the mellow summer sun had brought out many pedestrians and tourists who were enjoying the towpath and locks in a relaxed and festive mood. This was a great benefit, because these bystanders were only too eager to operate the locks, saving me the trouble of clambering in and out of my boat.

At the next lock I came upon, Town Lock, a family of four—mom and dad and two charming little girls—watched me pull up, and the father offered to work the lock for me. I passed the steel crank handle to him—with care, because if dropped it could punch a hole in the fabric of my craft—and sat back to enjoy the rise to a higher plane of life. One of the little girls, a doll of a child dressed in a pink and blue summer party dress and with blond locks glistening in the sun, watched me with wide-eyed awe as I rose to her level.

Thinking to impress her, and give her a story to tell her school-mates, I shouted, "I'm from America!"

"I'm from England!" she cried back, bold as brass.

"What's your name?"

"Olivia!"

"My name is Jim."

We smiled at each other for a few moments, and then I asked, "Can I take your picture?"

What happened next amazed me. I feared my question might produce uneasiness, or confusion, or a flight to mother—who was out of earshot at the other end of the lock. After all, how would you react if you were eight years old and some strange man from a foreign country, speaking in a foreign accent, asked to take your picture? Well, this child had no fear or shyness. She immediately dropped into a cute pose, tipping her head in her stylish, floppy white sun hat, as if she'd been working as a photographer's model for a baby food company all her life. And she held that pose for the many long seconds it took me to fumble my camera out of the bag and adjust it. I considered her poised, self-assured response to be strong evidence for my theory about English social confidence, and how English kids are stage-ready from birth.

I paddled away, reflecting on the charming encounter. The name *Olivia* has always held a certain magic for me. It's musical in itself, of course, but it is also the name of the leading character in Shakespeare's comic fantasy *Twelfth Night,* the first of the bard's plays I studied in the ninth grade—and long my favorite. The setting where Shakespeare's Olivia holds sway is the fairy-tale country of Illyria, a land of coincidence and mistaken identity, and as my journey unfolded, I began to feel I had entered an enchanted land myself.

A few miles farther along, I encountered another demonstration of English social confidence. When I reached the next lock, I found that I had caught up to several boats delayed by counter traffic through the lock. In addition to two narrowboats, the lock held a Thames skiff operated by three men obviously out on a holiday. Because bystanders were operating the lock for us, we remained in our boats. Once we had pulled into the lock and the heavy wooden gates had thudded closed behind us, I paddled over to the men in the skiff and began a conversation.

"So, it's three men in a boat, hey?" I said with a knowing chuckle.

They gave cheerful murmurs, indicating that they had caught my literary allusion.

English journalist Jerome K. Jerome had published the popular book titled *Three Men in a Boat* in 1889. It is an account of the comic adventures and mishaps of three effete urbanites who make a journey on the Thames in a rowing skiff. When I learned of it, I made a special effort to acquire a copy. It was a rather heavy hardback edition, not exactly suitable for my minimalist style of travel, but I was willing to make the sacrifice for a book so relevant to me, a fellow boater on the Thames.

My hopes were raised by the editor's introduction, which reported that the book is considered a gem of English literature, and is incredibly famous, having been printed and reprinted almost more than the Bible. The book's popularity springs partly from the timing of its original publication. It came out at the height of the Golden Age of the Thames, the period from 1870 to 1914, when the river became the pleasure ground for upper- and middle-class holidaymakers, most of whom thronged the water in Thames skiffs like the one Jerome wrote about.

The book is a work of deliberate, fictional humor that requires a particular funny bone to enjoy. The full title is *Three Men in a Boat (To Say Nothing of the Dog!)*. If that title cracks you up, this book is for you. Unfortunately, I did not have the requisite funny bone, and could not get past page 30. Several days after purchasing it, I discreetly left the heavy volume behind on the nightstand of my B&B in Windsor.

So when I met the men in the lock a few days later, the book was very much on my mind. After exchanging pleasantries, I returned to the topic. "You know, I've just been reading that book," I said, and I thereupon launched into a rather sweeping criticism of it, concluding, if I recall rightly, with the declaration that it was "pointless."

"So it didn't strike your fancy?" said one of the three men in a boat.

I smiled at his gentle understatement. "No, I guess you could say not."

We were all silent for a few moments, and then the conversation moved to other points. I asked them how long they were traveling, and they replied it would be a weekend voyage. They were intending to reach Godalming that night, a town four miles past Guildford, where they planned to stay in a B&B, and then make their way back to the Thames on Sunday. Then one of the crew, a short, stocky, balding man who had not said much up to that point, spoke.

"I think it's the greatest ever," he said in a firm, quiet tone.

I had no idea what he was talking about. Because he was standing facing half away from me, looking at the lock's wall when he said it, I wasn't sure whether he was talking to me or to himself.

"I beg your pardon?" I asked.

"That book."

"What book?"

"That one you were just talking about."

"Oh. You mean *Three Men in a Boat?*"

"Right. I think it's the greatest thing ever written." He said it perfectly calmly, without a trace of emotion.

"Really?" I replied. "Well . . . well, I mean, what do you like about it?"

"It's got everything: humor, philosophy, human nature. Everything you ever need to know is in that book."

"Really?" I said.

"Right," he continued. "That book . . . If I was to be on a desert island and could have just one book for the rest of my life, that'd be the book I'd have!"

There's a world of social significance in this little exchange. First, notice the power of courtesy at work. Alex politely held his peace while I savaged his favorite book. He refrained from contradicting me, and avoided starting an unfriendly argument. But then, notice the display of social confidence. Alex declared his fondness for the book as if standing on a stage, not concerned with how the audience—me—would likely receive his words. Actually, I was so impressed by his frank honesty that I was completely won over.

"Well, I guess I'll have to go back and read the book more carefully," I said after he had finished. (After I returned to the States, I bought another copy of *Three Men in a Boat,* and with the best will in the world tried to like it, but I have to report that the humor still eluded me.)

All the boats left the lock together, but I soon stopped to get out and photograph a scene of rhododendron bushes in bloom. Because I was moving more slowly than they to begin with, I assumed I had seen the last of them. Several hours later, I experienced the first of a series of coincidences that marked my excursion to Guildford.

This first connection was perhaps not so unexpected. I came upon their boat drawn up on the lawn of a canal-side pub where they had stopped for lunch. Though I'd already had my lunch—an energy bar—I disembarked to visit with them. During the visit, Alex explained that he lived near the Thames, in Hampton.

"I have a big, four-bedroom house there, and I'm rattling around in it by myself," he said. "You're welcome to come and stay if you like."

It was a wonderful invitation, because it would give me a place to stay while I visited Hampton Court Palace, Henry VIII's castle on the Thames. I planned to be there the following week, and I told him I would like to take up his offer. On the corner of my map, Alex wrote down his address, home phone, and mobile phone number—yet another demonstration of social confidence: being willing to invite a stranger who has just panned your favorite book to be a houseguest.

We chatted some more at a picnic table out in the sun, and then I said goodbye, heading to Guildford. Again, I expected to have seen the last of them on this canal journey.

The following morning, I was having breakfast at a restaurant in Guildford, seated at a table overlooking the canal. I glanced down at the water and noticed, at just that moment, my three men in a boat rowing past! I was to find out later that they had made very slow progress—being unable to withstand the enticements of pubs along the way—and had been forced to camp that night in a field several miles short of Guildford. Looking famished and disheveled, they seemed to be seeking a place to moor and breakfast. As it happened, I was in a position to help them solve both problems. I rushed outside and climbed up to a balcony overlooking the canal and called out. Once I got their attention, I explained where they could moor their skiff, and how to get up to the restaurant. They were quite surprised to see me, and happy to take my advice on both points. They soon joined me in the restaurant, and we had a pleasant visit over a full cooked English breakfast.

I could not but marvel at the coincidence of meeting Alex, David, and Trevor yet again, especially given my haphazard travel patterns. If we had planned a rendezvous, I doubt we could have accomplished it, considering everything that could have gone wrong. But on this trip I had left my social schedule in the hands of the gods, and, time after time, they apparently knew how to resolve the equations of space and time to make everything come out right.

11

Expressions of Faith

Now we must step back in time, to the previous afternoon when I left Alex and his friends having lunch on the pub's lawn. For before that day was over, I was drawn into a separate subplot, one that involved different characters and a fascinating side of English life.

I had made no preparations about where to stay or what to do about my boat: Guildford was a completely unknown entity. When I pulled into the city, it was much later than I had intended, already getting dark. My first problem was finding a secluded, safe place to leave my boat. As I approached the center of the city over the last two miles, I was on careful lookout for a mooring option—a marina, a boat club, or, ideally, a B&B with a dock on the water—but nothing of the sort appeared. Nor did I see any pedestrian whom I could ask about lodging and mooring possibilities. Nor were there any stairways to get to the street level, which was 10 feet above the canal level. The canal ran through a seedy, industrial part of town—I smelled sewage for the first time on my trip—and I faced stone walls on both sides, blank and silent.

Eventually, I reached the heart of town where the canal stood naked to the streets and pedestrian walkways. There I found a stone stairway running up the side of the canal wall, and I took advantage of it to moor the kayak and climb up to ground level. It was a rough neighborhood, crowded with pubs that were booming at this early Saturday evening hour, their inebriated customers spilling out onto the streets, pushing and shoving one another, usually in a good-natured way, but sometimes with hostility. It seemed the worst possible place to leave the boat overnight. What chance, I wondered, would a little canvas kayak stand in this hostile environment?

But I had no alternative. I couldn't wrestle the kayak up the stairs by myself. And even if I was able to haul it to street level and disassembled it, I couldn't lug the pack around with me as I hiked miles around the city searching for lodging.

I learned from a passerby that there was a hotel at Angel Gate on the High Street, and I headed in the direction he indicated. Soon, as inevitably happens on the twisting English streets, I was lost and had to seek directions again. However, asking strangers for assistance at this time and place was something of a challenge, because pedestrians had their minds on other things. No one seemed in the mood to make a connection with a stranger.

The street was populated, in the main, by young women strutting in groups of twos and threes, decked out for a Saturday night's fortune hunting. In England, young women wear skirts quite high, but on this special party night, the hemline of their gold lamé and white satin miniskirts was hiked an additional 1 5/8 inches, revealing such a frightening amount of thigh that it didn't seem legal to look. The girls were like models, tipping along in high spiky heels, with their abundant, flowing hair, radiant blush painted on lip and cheek, and eyelashes like flyswatters. They were interesting to look at, but they seemed to exist in a parallel universe. I felt that if I asked one of them for directions to the hotel, she would walk straight through me.

Then I spotted a young woman who was different. She had short, straight, dark brown hair and was dressed in ordinary dark slacks. She was not like the models with eyes focused at middle distance. She was looking at the people she encountered, open to connection, and when our eyes met, I was prompted to ask my question.

Anna was eager to help, and began by detailing directions to the Angel Hotel. In the middle of giving me these directions, she realized they were too complicated for me to follow. "I'll take you there," she concluded.

As we walked down the street, she asked where I was from and what I was up to, and I explained my kayak trip down the Thames, and the diversion to Guildford on the Wey Navigation. I also mentioned that I had left the boat in a highly insecure location down at the canal and was worried about it.

"What is your name?" she asked. I told her.

"Then I will pray for the safety of your kayak, Jim."

My ears pricked up at this comment. In England, interest in religion has been declining precipitously, a decline that has hit the official Church of England especially hard. Three centuries ago, it was the only recognized church, and everyone was required to attend it. Today, in the age of religious tolerance and modern distractions, less than 2 percent of the population regularly attends its services. Every year, more C of E church buildings are closed and sold off. In the town of Eton, I visited one chapel that had been taken over for use by the National Health Service bureaucracy—a creepy touch worthy of Orwell. The C of E churches that continue to function are hardly outgoing, but concentrate on ritual performed out of sight in echoing stone buildings.

Given the secular background in England, it was quite surprising to encounter a person who had the idea of prayer at the forefront of her mind when meeting a stranger on the street.

"What church do you go to?" I asked.

Not any organized church, she replied. She belonged to an informal Christian group, called the Boiler Room, which met in private homes.

"Is it possible to attend their gatherings?" I asked. We had, by this time, reached the entrance to the Angel's Gate Hotel.

"Will you still be in Guildford tomorrow?" she asked. I nodded. "Then I'll meet you here at 12:15, and take you there."

After passing the night at the YMCA hostel (the Angel's Gate Hotel proved to be crushingly expensive), I rushed out to the street the next morning, and walked quickly down to the canal to see what had become of my poor little kayak. In these situations—early morning of a new day, with the kayak left in an insecure mooring—I found myself humming the line from the *Star Spangled Banner* about how the "dawn's early light gave proof through the night that our flag was still there." And yes, in this case—aided by the wings of Anna's prayer—the kayak "was still there." As I approached it, I found a man on the pavement above staring down at it with extreme curiosity. When I explained to him that it was my kayak, he was very friendly and interested in my trip, so I'm sure he was more of an ally and protector than any kind of threat to it.

Not wishing to risk exposing the boat another night, I spent the morning paddling through another lock and a mile farther up the canal to the Guildford Rowing Club, which the desk clerk at the Y had suggested as a safe place to leave the boat. The volunteers at the rowing club were very understanding, and helped me stow the boat in a secure spot behind some racing shells.

At 12:15, I was waiting at the Angel Gate. Anna came up through the crowd, bringing her clean-cut, quiet boyfriend along. After introductions, we walked along the curving streets until we reached a modest house on the Chertsey Road. Stan and Melinda welcomed us in after we rang the bell. Stan had been a Christian missionary in Yugoslavia for several years before settling in Guildford. I was introduced to other members, about a dozen young adults who had gathered for a potluck lunch. It was an extremely convivial group, and everyone fell into prolonged conversations, which delayed lunch for several hours. I hardly noticed the passage of time because I, too, became engrossed talking with others. I spent the better part of an hour learning about the life history of Kera, a 30-year-old Canadian woman who had uprooted herself—against the wishes of her parents—to further her Christian faith by going abroad. After visiting several places in Europe, she had joined this Boiler Room group, and had for the time being settled in Guildford.

I asked several people to tell me about the Boiler Room, but I have to confess I came away with no very definite picture. It is not a formal organization, and does not have any official leaders. Someone said the movement began in the United States, but it appears to be international, with units in South Africa, Spain, and Germany, among other places. It is composed almost entirely of young people. Although members speak of working on behalf of social justice, the poor, and the environment, the movement does not look to political action to pursue these goals. Instead, the focus is personal, with members emphasizing fellowship, friendship, and prayer. The movement has Christian roots, and makes reference to verses in the Bible—in both the Old and New Testaments—but it is nondenominational and open, and pays little attention to theology beyond the basic injunction to "Love thy neighbor." Some of the units are tied in with churches, or at least operate out of church buildings; others are storefront or home-based.

The Boiler Room is closely related to a movement called 24-7 Prayer, which apparently began at a prayer vigil in Chichester, England, in 1999. As the name implies, the 24-7 movement develops prayer rooms that are continuously open. After grasping this Guildford group's emphasis on prayer, I understood why Anna's first thought when I met her on the street the previous night was to pray for the safety of my kayak.

Later in the afternoon, after we had eaten lunch and the excitement of conversation calmed, the group gathered in the living room for a worship service, which consisted of a single Psalm read by Melinda. After a few moments of silence, Stan, the host, opened discussion by asking the group to consider "how we can move our commitment to the next level." After considerable discussion, the group decided to try having regular, brief morning prayer sessions at 7:30 a.m. in different homes, where a Celtic prayer would be read. They also liked the idea Stan proposed of everyone saying the Lord's Prayer at exactly noon, wherever they happen to be.

Then members discussed how they might share love with friends and neighbors, and further the sense of community. Their thinking continued to ways of giving moral support to others through friendship, mentoring, and prayer; no one mentioned material assistance such as food or money. One idea someone proposed, which fit their style of emphasizing personal and emotional support, was to join with the "Night Angels" program in Guildford. These are Christian activists who, on Friday and Saturday nights, circulate in the rough downtown pub area—the place where I left my kayak—and meet people emerging in troubled states from the pubs. Their mission is to befriend the lonely, distressed, and chemically ill, and guide them away from self-destructive behavior. Police records show a significant drop in evening crime incidents since the Night Angels have become active.

When Stan asked me for any thoughts I might have about the group, I suggested that perhaps they should have some way of identifying themselves to the public—something like a button or wrist band. My idea was that this external symbol might be a way to advertise their group and recruit new members. "You're going about on the streets of Guildford doing good works," I said. "Shouldn't people know what lies behind your actions, what it connects to?"

"I don't see the point of that," said Stan. "I mean, what would it add? We are who we are. We don't have to advertise it."

His reaction revealed that I had somewhat misunderstood the nature of the group. I was adopting a purpose-oriented perspective, thinking that the group's objective was to *achieve* something. In this perspective, the world would be a better place if there were more Boiler Room followers, more helpers like Anna to assist lost travelers. Therefore, I assumed, the group should take steps to increase its numbers, like gaining public recognition and becoming better organized.

I began to see that the people around me in that living room were not oriented toward typical measures of success, not even success in good works. Their meeting together and the helpful actions they might take in their daily lives were an expression of their own spiritual needs. They weren't interested in recruiting new members. They felt that if it was right for others to join them, God would bring them along.

Toward evening, the Boiler Room group began to break up. In parting, Stan gave me a copy of his book. It was a slender, lovingly designed and illustrated volume on the lives of saints. I promised to send him my book of kayak adventures when I got home. I made my way down the street and back to my room at the YMCA, marveling at this nucleus of healthy spiritual and social energy I was privileged to witness.

I could not help but contrast this gathering with my visit to Guildford Cathedral the following day. This cathedral is the newest in the country, construction begun in 1933 and completed in 1966. It is grandly sited atop a hill at the edge of the city and can be seen from the countryside for miles around. The building itself is rather drab, with modern, unembellished lines, and constructed of dull, dark brown bricks.

In the late afternoon, I hiked up to the building to hear the choral evensong service, and sat in the front row. Before me, on both sides of the chancel, was a choir of some 30 men and boys, decked out in white and scarlet gowns. Seated farther back were the clergy and wardens, also opulently garbed in sweeping, flowing robes. I went there mainly to hear the music—which was wonderful, of course—but the service itself was entirely ritual. Every word—scripture, chants, and songs—had been laid down by others, decades, centuries, even millennia ago. The entire service could have been conducted by robots. The only genuine human behavior on view was the occasional fidgeting and suppressed byplay among the choirboys.

What a contrast this made with the Boiler Room group, where, except for the brief reading of the Psalm, the gathering consisted entirely of spontaneous human exchanges!

Another contrast, which says a great deal about the direction the official Church of England is heading, was in the attendance. In Melinda's living room on Chertsey Road, there were 12 of us. In the entire 1,000-seat nave of the Guildford cathedral that evening, there were but five congregants, including me. If you want to hear the sound of lonely, listen to the footfalls of five people echoing beneath great stone arches in a cathedral of a religion that used to be popular.

To complete the thread of this tale about Anna and the Boiler Room group, we must jump ahead 10 days to a scene in London.

Being plunged into the middle of this great city was quite a shock for me after my relaxed exploration of the placid Thames. I know that, in theory, urbanization brings economic and cultural advantages, but upon first facing the stressful bustle of London, my dominant thought was that God did not intend mankind to live in cities—a sentiment I perhaps picked up from Thames-side philosophers William Morris and Tom Rolt, who both deplored the dehumanizing effect of urban life.

The intense traffic on London's narrow streets feels highly dangerous, especially for an American who finds cars coming from an unexpected direction. And nobody seems to know anything about the place because everyone's a tourist. London has little sense of community; even the clerks in the stores don't know about their area because they live elsewhere. They cannot tell you if there's a library down the street, and they don't know that Mozart composed his first symphony in a house around the corner.

The sidewalks are narrow and crowded, so pedestrians are in constant competition with one another as they push their way along; everyone, perhaps understandably, seems to live in his or her own private space, not taking any interest in the environment, not looking at others, not reaching out.

My kayak voyage had progressed to the middle of London, and I again had to leave the boat tethered in a most precarious situation on the river, down by the Prince Albert Bridge. I had finally managed to find a hotel and was pushing through the bustling pedestrian traffic looking for a place to eat supper when I spotted an anomaly: a pedestrian who was thoughtfully looking at the world!

She was a young woman bearing a large rucksack on her back who was positively sauntering, stopping to peer at buildings, even turning herself in a complete circle while gazing up at the buildings. In rushing, nose-to-the-grindstone London, she stood out like a butterfly in a beehive. I tried to guess why she was taking such a deep interest in her surroundings, and came up with the idea that she was looking for a hotel—because that was what I had just finished doing. I thought I might be able to help her by sharing my findings, so I crossed the street to greet her. "Are you looking for a hotel?" I asked.

When a young woman is accosted by a strange man in a big city, she is likely to be guarded, even startled. In any case, she would be inclined to limit the interaction. But not Missie. She gave me an open smile, as if I were a friend she already knew.

"No," she said with a little laugh.

"Well, I saw you looking around and I was wondering what you were looking for . . . ?"

"It's just so fascinating! All this," she said, waving her arm at the buildings. "It's so amazing." She seemed breathless, exhilarated, like a skier just finishing a run.

She went on to explain that she wasn't looking for lodgings because she planned to take a flight later that evening. We immediately fell into a conversation about our backgrounds and plans. She was from Taunton, in Somerset; I told her that my wife and I had lived near there, in Exmouth, some years ago. She was heading for a weeklong retreat in Macedonia and had many hours to kill before her late-night flight. I asked her what was in the huge backpack she was struggling with. Clothes, she said.

"But I've been living on the Thames for a month," I said, "and my pack is one-tenth that size. For example, I have just this one shirt I'm wearing. How many shirts do you have?"

She giggled. "I packed nine blouses."

Nine blouses for seven days! I had trouble wrapping my mind around such a number.

We were so much enjoying each other's company that I invited her to have supper with me. After spending nearly two hours at the Shakespeare restaurant by Victoria Station, we decided to release the table for other customers and removed to a nearby pub, where I had a hot chocolate and she ordered herbal tea (she insisted on paying, in exchange for supper).

Missie was a handsome woman, age 25, with long, wavy chestnut hair. She worked as a sales assistant in an upscale home furnishings store. She said she felt a little guilty about participating in this shallow, materialistic side of life because her heart and soul were elsewhere. She had traveled quite widely, and had been married for a time while living in Canada. Her husband proved to be extremely overbearing and chauvinistic, so she had to escape from that relationship. It came out that she was a Christian, and had made a number of trips to different parts of the world—California, Yugoslavia, India—to participate in Christian retreats.

I asked if she attended any particular church. She replied *no*; she was not interested in formal church membership or regular church services. She was, she said, active in a group called the Boiler Room, which had started in Kansas City. My ears pricked up.

"I know about that," I said. "I went to a meeting of a Boiler Room group in Guildford. It was led by a person named Stan. . . ."

Missie's eyes opened wide. "You know Stan?!" she asked.

"Is it the same person?" I asked. "His wife is Melinda, and they have two little children. . . ."

"Trevor and Elizabeth," she finished. I nodded. "That's amazing!" she said. "It was Stan who introduced me to the Boiler Room.

I met him several years ago in Yugoslavia when he was doing missionary work there." She shook her head in disbelief. "So how did you find out about the Boiler Room in Guildford?"

"It's really odd," I said. "By accident, I met a woman on the street in Guildford that I got to know, and she took me to their meeting. Her name was Anna. . . ."

Missie's mouth dropped. "You met Anna??!! That's amazing! Anna is my best friend! I've known her for years!" Then after a pause she asked, "How could that be, that you met Anna?"

We talked some more about the Boiler Room, and then it was time for Missie to make her way to Heathrow. I accompanied her through the maze of Victoria Station until we found the entrance to the underground, where we hugged goodbye.

For days afterward, I pondered the coincidence of our meeting, attempting to discern the mystical force operating beneath the surface of things that connected Anna, Missie, and me. It's not as though the two of them lived in the same little English village that I happened to visit. I met Anna in Guildford and I met Missie days later and miles away on the streets of London with its eight million people.

But perhaps the link with Anna and Missie was not just coincidence. They did have something in common that set them apart from the masses who rush along city streets fixed on their narrow purposes. They were curious about the world; they were looking at the people around them, open to connection. As such, perhaps they comprised a special subgroup of aware seekers—a village as it were—whose members are likely to bump into one another. If, years from now, I am walking city streets somewhere and encounter the one person from among the busy thousands who actually looks back at me and starts a conversation, I have a feeling she could be a friend of Anna's and Missie's.

12

Departing Illyria

When William the Conqueror did what he is known so well for doing, namely conquering England in 1066, he was understandably and deservedly unpopular. He and his men couldn't go out at night because the dispossessed English were inclined to hurl sticks and stones—and even sharper, deadlier items—at them. So he built a string of castles where he could retire in the evening, put his feet up, and feel safe from English arrows. The Norman invaders were prodigious castle builders, erecting a new one about every two weeks, so that after 20 years, there were some 500 all across England. The most famous of these castles are the Tower of London and Windsor Castle. Both of these structures have been kept in use over the years, and have been expanded and upgraded so they feel rather modern and distant from the warring times of a thousand years ago.

This has not been the case with Guildford Castle. Built soon after the 1066 invasion, it early on served as a royal residence and center of administration, but was later abandoned after kings shifted their attention to other castles. After sitting idle for several centuries, the ruined castle was bought in 1611 by a Guildford merchant who had the idea of making it a private residence—surely the mother of all fixer-uppers! However, stone, damp, and mold resisted his efforts, and the castle remained what it is today . . . a ruin. Local authorities have done enough repairs to allow tourists to prowl around the old structure, so I was able to climb the winding stone stairway to the top of the tower and survey the surrounding country, imagining myself in the shoes of the nervous Norman conquerors. The restorers have converted the castle's moat into a supremely graceful park and flower garden where retired folk sit and feed the pigeons—thus putting his bellicose structure to a use that William never could have imagined.

After four days of sightseeing and visiting in Guildford, I was ready to retrace my route along the Wey Navigation and return to the Thames. The main difference in the return journey was that I made it not on the weekend but on a Wednesday, when there were no helpful gongoozlers hanging around the canal to operate the locks for me. I had to do everything myself at each of the 10 locks: getting in and out of the kayak three times, opening and closing gates twice, and opening and closing sluices twice. The worst part was climbing down the little rickety iron ladder to reach and board the kayak at the bottom of the drained lock. It was impossibly dangerous to attempt this descent while carrying the sluice crank handle. My solution was to set the crank at the edge of the canal downstream and collect it after leaving the lock.

In the early afternoon, I reached Cambridge Wharf, a little hamlet that had a pub and some picnic tables alongside the canal, and I stopped to rest and snack on an energy bar. The place was deserted except for one man who was meandering about in a most peculiar manner. Almost everyone along the canal rather quickly fits into a known category: walkers, workmen, boaters, businessmen taking a break, local tourists, foreign tourists, and so on. Well, this man fit in no category, and his behavior was quite inexplicable.

He was about 50, rather tall, dressed casually, but rather pointedly so, and had what looked like a cowboy jacket neatly folded over his arm. He was slowly pacing to and fro, smoking a cigarette, stopping to scuff the dirt with his toe, occasionally sitting on the bench of a picnic table for a few moments. He brought to my mind that famous line from Keats:

> Oh what can ail thee, knight-at-arms,
> Alone and palely loitering?

He appeared to be waiting for something, but not at all eagerly. He was not looking at the surroundings, and was avoiding eye contact—suggesting he was averse to meeting anyone. He had brought nothing to amuse himself—no book, newspaper, or cell phone. His face was haggard and sad. If there had been a cliff or a high bridge nearby, I would have suspected he was contemplating suicide. Since there wasn't, I couldn't for the life of me guess what had brought him to this place.

After some time, when I was about to get back in the kayak and continue my trip, a van pulled up, people clambered out, and before I knew it, they were setting up a TV camera alongside the canal, aiming downstream. Was something newsworthy about to happen? I asked a young woman holding a clipboard what was going on.

"We're shooting footage for a TV comedy," she said.

"What's the show?" I asked.

"It's for the satellite network," she continued, giving a channel number that meant nothing to me. "The working title is *On the Water with Rich and Jo*. You know, Rich Hall and Jo Brand?"

My face remained blank.

"The comedians, Rich and Jo. That's Rich over there," she said, pointing to the palely loitering knight. "Surely you've heard of him. He's American."

The announcement that the man I had pegged as a potential suicide victim was a famous comedian was hard to believe. More people came to the canal side, including the director and an assistant director, and a second camera crew who set themselves up on top of the bridge crossing the canal. I found out more about the project from another staffer, who spoke in almost reverent terms about Rich Hall. I have since learned that he is one of the leading comedians in Britain, having played his grouchy, American hillbilly persona on BBC-2, at the Edinburgh Festival, the Sheffield Festival, in the Sydney Opera House, on the *Late Show with David Letterman,* and so on. His shows have included, *How the West was Lost, The Rich Hall Fishing Show,* and—a title that seemed strikingly appropriate—*Hell No I Ain't Happy.* He's also written nine books of humor and comic tales.

For the segment being filmed on this day, Rich and Jo were making a trip up the Wey Navigation in a canal boat. Rich had come ahead to Cambridge Wharf to await the boat that was carrying Jo.

Sure enough, the narrowboat eventually arrived, and Jo, a portly woman wearing a bright red wraparound wool skirt, disembarked, and the crews shot footage of her pulling on the mooring rope, while big, fluffy outdoor microphones recorded her banter with Rich.

When the mooring was completed, the director came over to me. He was tall, thin as a reed, very young, seemingly just out of college.

"Is that your kayak there?"

"Oh, is it in the way?" I asked. "Do you want me to move it?"

"No, no. It's perfectly fine," he said. "What I was wondering—if it's all right with you—is whether you might possibly let us borrow it for a few minutes to get some shots of Rich in it."

The question rather threw me for a second, because I'd never had any dealings with celebrities. I wasn't worried about the kayak, but what if Rich got hurt? He probably knew nothing at all about being in a kayak.

"Of course, it's completely up to you," continued the director, "so if you're not comfortable about it or anything . . . ?"

What decided it for me was the Klepper's beautiful stability. Even the klutziest person could not turn it over. "Well, sure," I said.

To make things as easy as possible, I spent a few minutes unloading the bow section so Rich would have room for his lanky legs. When I finished piling what seemed like all my worldly possessions on the bank of the canal, the director, who was observing me, said in his cultured Oxford accent and with a twinkle in his eye, "Actually, this is just an elaborate ruse to steal your kayak."

I laughed heartily. This filming operation, involving two camera and sound crews, half a dozen staffers, the stars, and the rented, highly polished narrowboat and its crew, likely cost more per minute than my faded red canvas kayak was worth.

Rich stepped off the canal edge and struggled to get into the kayak. He showed no sense of balance, and if the craft had been narrower, I think he might have overturned. But the sturdy Klepper forgave his missteps, and he was soon safely seated and experimenting with the paddle, making himself glide down the canal. I took a picture of the cameraman filming him paddling in my boat—against the sun.

"Isn't that a no-no?" I asked the cameraman. "To shoot against the sun?"

"We do it all the time," he said.

I was under no illusions that this scene with my kayak would appear on nationwide TV. The cameraman told me that for each segment of the show, they film about 10 hours of scenes and end up using 10 minutes in the final version.

Rich made it back to his starting point, but with the same grim expression on his face: The kayak ride had obviously done nothing to lift his spirits. He climbed out of the boat, and then noticed some lettering on the bow, which he inspected with interest. The yellow vinyl letters Rich was looking at said "SANDPOINT * ID." I had put them on the boat years ago, just before I set out on my trip up the Hudson River in 2004. My fantasy was that some day, at some marina or dock, a stranger would notice them and exclaim, "Oh, are you from Sandpoint!?" and that would be the beginning of an interesting connection.

Well, it never happened, not on the Hudson River trip, nor on the Saint Lawrence River, nor on the trip to Key West, nor on the Mississippi, the Connecticut, or the Chattahoochee. All over America, these tiny letters had been ignored—until that afternoon in faraway England.

"Oh," said Rich, "are you from Sandpoint?"

"Yes," I said eagerly. "Have you heard of it?"

"I go through there all the time. Nice little town."

"How come you know about it?"

"I live in Livingston, Montana, just across the border."

"No kidding?!" I said, "What a coincidence to meet a neighbor so far from home! There's a big rail yard there in Livingston, isn't there?" He nodded. "I spent a day there once, taking pictures of the engines," I explained.

We chatted some more, and then I said goodbye, to continue down the canal. As we shook hands in parting, I felt impelled to give him a word of encouragement, for our conversation had done nothing to dispel my impression that he was carrying some kind of burden.

"Now you cheer up now, y'hear?" I don't think he attributed any special significance to my words, but I hoped they might work unconsciously to brighten his outlook.

At the time, I thought it bizarre that I should be attempting to raise the mood of a professional comedian. In theory, comedians are supposed to be the happy people who cheer up the rest of us. But I have since studied some clips of Rich's—and also of Jo Brand—and realized that most of their humor—and perhaps that of many other modern comedians—emphasizes sad, hostile, and sarcastic themes. One of Rich's lines is that he came from a hill-billy family "so poor that blues singers used to call round when they had writer's block." So perhaps being a comedian isn't such a jolly life after all.

The ruins of the Newark Priory stand alongside the Wey Canal near the village of Pyrford. I had spotted the crumbling stone walls on my way up to Guildford the previous Saturday, and at that time had formed in my mind the idea—a subtle but strangely impelling desire—that I should camp there overnight on my way back to the Thames. After leaving Rich and the TV crew, I reached the area in the late afternoon and set about turning this ambition into reality.

I stopped at the road bridge near the priory and climbed up to see what I could learn about it. A placard explained that it was an establishment of the Augustinian Order, consisting of a cathedral and other buildings built in the 12th century. After thriving for 400 years, it was dissolved by Henry VIII in the 16th century, as part of his campaign to stamp out Catholicism. The buildings had been abandoned, and over the following centuries, the facing stones were pilfered to use elsewhere, leaving walls of rough, undressed stones. Time has somewhat ravaged the walls, but even after 500 years of neglect, much of the structure remains—minus, of course, anything made of wood, including the roofs. Two sides of the cathedral are still intact, with the walls standing some 40 to 50 feet high.

The priory ruins stood in a cow pasture, which was enclosed along the road by a barbed-wire fence. A sign there said "Private Land No Entry," and that was enough to discourage me from trying to reach the ruins from that direction. But I was not about to give up. I returned to the kayak and paddled farther along the canal, and put myself through the next lock. Below it, I found a tongue of the Wey River that extended toward the ruins.

I paddled up this inlet and was able to draw within 100 yards of the priory, alongside a bank that had no fence blocking my way, nor any sign discouraging entry. So in the unlikely event that anyone should challenge my presence, I could confidently assert that I had violated no barrier and transgressed no injunction.

This episode proved, once again, that when it comes to sneaking into places where you probably aren't supposed to be, there really is no substitute for a kayak. I waited for dusk, and then unloaded my camping gear and carried it over to the ruins. What happened next is perhaps best conveyed by the poem I was prompted to write about the experience:

In Priory Ruins

In setting sun through willow's fluff I spied
The jagged walls of once a mighty chapel
Standing tall, despite a thousand winters tried,
Amidst the cows and thistles side by side.

Since soul nor house nor fence stood in the way
Of ancient love and spirit, I did resolve
Where brown-robed monks would early chant and pray
To spend the night and see what walls would say.

I soft explore beneath a sky all red
Doors, and sills, and arches hardly safe,
And find a flat among the stones long dead;
There with care to spread my cloth and bed.

Sky fades, night comes, and snuggle I alone.
Eyes close a bit, then open more to see
In wall opposed two eyes alike my own
Of empty arches sprung in curvéd stone.

And more: a nose between, and brows above,
A face indeed: could be the face of God
Quiet stood, and patient thinking of
Some way to tell deaf mortals of His love.

Some moments on I saw what I thought odd,
A flashing speck that crept within the arch:
A plane! To grasp its sign I lacked no prod:
Precious lives a glint in eye of God.

What if—I asked the face—to live may need
A dream so rare and so unlikely filled
That thoughtful seeker know if reason heed
No vital key can drop, whate'er I plead?

The question hung in space before the face.
Then answer came: "Believe in miracles!"
From Him, or me, or sky I cannot trace
Whence sprung so simple logic in that place.

13

In Tyrant's Den

I woke early in my nest at the priory ruins—my sleep being shortchanged, as usual, by the cold—and made my way across the pasture to the kayak as soon as there was enough light to avoid stepping on cow pies. The whole world was still sleeping, and the only sound disturbing the mist came from chirping birds as I glided over the glassy water. In what seemed like no time at all, I made it to Weybridge back on the Thames, only to find that Carrie, the lockkeeper, was not yet on duty at the canal headquarters. I moored the kayak above the first lock and went into town for breakfast at the same Italian café I had visited on my way up the canal the previous Saturday, and ordered, again, a sausage baguette. (See how easy it is to start a breakfast tradition in England!)

The day before I left Guildford, I had phoned Alex about staying at his house in Hampton. This town lies right next to the tourist highlight I planned to visit, Hampton Court, the opulent palace of King Henry VIII. Alex explained that he would be away in London the following day for a job interview, but he gave me detailed instructions for making myself at home.

I found the inlet off the river that led to the rowing club where he told me I could leave the kayak. The launching ramp there was guarded by hissing swans anxious to protect their one little cygnet, and I had to splash and shout at them for some time before they gave way. I heaved the boat out of the water and carried it across the grass to a safe spot behind some rowing shells. With directions from several pedestrians, I found Alex's house, located the door key under the second dustbin, and let myself in. After unpacking and trying a few notes on his piano—which was remarkably well in tune—I left the house and headed for Hampton Court, which lay a mile's walk downriver.

As I approached the palace, uneasiness began to overtake me—an anxiety that rather caught me off guard. It concerned the historical bloodshed of Tudor days. Normally, I'm able to treat ancient violence casually, as if it were some distant, practically fictional event. I could view the suffering and horrors as not happening to real people, but as some kind of cartoon—a Wiley Coyote episode in which characters repeatedly go splat, but are never injured. I think we all do this to some degree—and we must do it to keep our sanity. But on occasion, when I make physical contact with the artifacts of a historical wrong, the outrages of yesteryear seem real and disturbing to me. This kind of historical time traveling came upon me as I faced the brick and stone of Henry VIII's actual palace. I began to feel a little bit irate at the man, and irritated with the world for not being as upset with him as I was.

Henry was, by modern standards, a monster. You name it, he did it. Genocide was all in a day's work: He ordered mass, indiscriminant slayings in Yorkshire after the revolt there in 1537. Murder—legal murder—of court officials was his stock in trade. He killed some 40 high administrators and friends (former friends!)—vastly more than any other English ruler. In addition to these gruesome excesses, Henry implemented the bizarre horror of putting to death a wife—that is, the human being he loved and shared a bed with. Doing this just one time would be a dreadful stain; Henry did it twice to prove to everybody he really knew how.

Henry is now somewhat honored for breaking England away from the Catholic Church, but a close look at that action brings no credit to the man. Henry didn't decide through study and introspection that papal rule was morally or spiritually unsound. He simply wanted to ditch a first wife and publicly marry another, and the Catholic pope said no. So Henry canceled that church and started a new one that said yes. Henry's new church added nothing of spirituality or tenderness to the life of England. It was as happily vicious as the old one: 26 people were burned for heresy in the last eight years of his reign.

This wasn't the first time I had experienced an emotional reaction to Henry VIII. Fifty years earlier, as a student at Highgate, the boarding school in north London, I made a visit to the Tower of London. I was at first enjoying my tour, pleasantly impressed by the sturdy stone walls, and awed by the portly Beefeaters in their bright red uniforms. Then, while walking around the courtyard, I spotted a polished wooden block off to one side, and went to inspect it. A shiny brass plate said that this was a replica of the cherry wood block on which the executioner had cut off Anne Boleyn's head! The scene was much too real for me—the vision of this woman having her head sliced off, and it rolling onto the grass, her wide eyes staring into the sky. For days afterward, I felt sick thinking how anyone could do such a thing, and especially how Henry could do it to his wife.

So, to put it mildly, I was in a bad mood as I walked along the sandy grit of the walkway to the palace, not at all disposed to be an appreciative tourist. Perhaps I should have turned around and gone back to Alex's, but inertia—and also a sense of touristic obligation—carried me forward. Everyone said Hampton Court Palace was a sight to see, perhaps the most splendid expression of art, architecture, and gardens in all of England, and it didn't seem sensible to let my emotional mood of the moment stop me from seeing it.

I paid my £16 and entered the visitor's hall. Examining the history and description material in the glass cases, I learned that even the origins of the palace were tainted with violence. The placard explained that Henry played no role in creating it. The building was constructed at the instigation of Thomas Wolsey, Henry's lord chancellor and right-hand man. In one of his typical acts of greedy double-cross, Henry accused Wolsey of treason and took the palace away from him (Wolsey died of natural causes before he could be executed).

An elderly English couple was standing next to me reading the same placard. They seemed relaxed and calm, fully pleased to be in this grand building, and I couldn't resist voicing my thoughts.

"Whew," I said after reading the paragraph. "Wasn't he terrible!?"

The man turned to me. "What do you mean?"

"Henry VIII. I mean, the guy was a murderer, right?"

He regarded me with a gentle smile, as though trying to calm me, "Oh, well, weren't they all in those days?"

That didn't, to my mind, excuse anybody, but I could see I wasn't going to get an argument from such a polite couple. "Yes, I suppose so," I said.

The guidebooks say that it's impossible to see everything at Hampton Court—especially because it's been enlarged after Henry's day with additions by the celebrated architect Christopher Wren—so I decided to let myself wander and encounter whatever fragments came to view. My feet brought me first to the royal kitchens—room after room of tall, whitewashed walls and huge walk-in fireplaces big enough to roast whole cows.

If you don't like someone, your opinion of him will not be raised by learning about his food supply, by learning how nature's delicate flora and fauna are crushed, seared, and mangled beyond recognition for the purpose of adding to his corpulence. In the case of Henry VIII, and the thousand flatterers and flunkies surrounding him at Hampton Court, there was a lot of corpulence requiring sustenance. Records of those days reveal that in one year, 1,240 oxen and 8,200 sheep were cooked in these kitchens. The tourists happily milling about the kitchens seemed entirely unaware of this slaughter, a consumption that amounted to 3.4 oxen and 22.5 sheep a day. I thought it was a point vegetarians ought to ponder.

And of course, the food wasn't donated voluntarily by peasants from the surrounding countryside as a token of their esteem. These peasants were taxed, pushed to the brink of starvation by soldiers who seized their stock and crops so that the king's friends might eat heartily. I wondered why socialists hadn't made a point of this. Oh, and these friends consumed 600,000 gallons of beer yearly, which works out to be 13.1 pints of beer a day per person. These people must have been so busy drinking there was hardly any time left in the day for bearbaiting, cockfighting, and declaring war on other countries, but they managed to fit it all in.

Thoroughly depressed by the kitchens, I climbed to the royal apartments on the upper floors. Visually, this was a huge improvement over the bare, rough caverns below. These state rooms are lavishly decorated with paintings on the walls, paintings on the ceilings, and elaborately carved designs wherever there was wood to bear them. However, I did not escape the looming ghost of the place, for instead of merely confronting what Henry ate, I came face to face with . . . Henry himself! Yes, there he was, dressed just like his picture, in light blue tights, white ermine-trimmed robe with floppy sleeves, Renaissance hat, and a jewel-studded pendant hanging in front of his rotund midriff. Of course he was an actor, and so were the other court members he was addressing. I had stumbled onto a bit of theater that the management puts on throughout the day in the palace. In this tableau, I was seeing a reenactment of the wedding day of Henry and his third wife, Jane Seymour. The actors were ad-libbing their parts, acting very naturally and convincingly.

Henry was in a booming expansive mood, bragging about his new wife. "See how beautiful she is!" he said, sweeping his arm toward Jane. "I think she's the most beautiful woman in the kingdom, don't you?" The courtiers murmured assent.

Then Henry directed his attention to one of the officials standing by, chiding him for having a dispute with another official. "I'm sure you will find a way to do better in future, now won't you?" Henry concluded. I couldn't tell what the other tourists were thinking—about 25 of us were watching this impromptu performance—but I sensed sharp steel behind the velvet.

For most of the performance, my eyes were riveted on Jane because I knew what must have been going through her mind. She had been a lady-in-waiting for Anne Boleyn, Henry's second wife. Jane had probably double-crossed Anne by slipping into Henry's bed on those slow nights when there weren't any executions to take care of. Anne had been beheaded just 11 days before this wedding, and the smell of blood was in the air. You knew Jane was wondering if she would be next. When the king looked at her and praised her, she glowed with pride and confidence, but when his gaze went elsewhere, she would turn and throw a worried glance at her lady-in-waiting.

This dramatic tableau was about all of Henry VIII that I could stand for the day. When it was over, I headed for the exit, walking quickly past vast artistic treasures.

With a sigh of relief, I gained the fresh air and open sky outside and found myself in the formal gardens. Acres and acres of gardens were laid out in a very spacious and industrial way, which, for this pilgrim, lacked voice or personality. I was determined to see and experience one item in the garden, however: the famous Hampton Court Maze. It's just like those little puzzles in children's books where you're supposed to trace a line from beginning to end, only this maze is made of hornbeam hedges standing 15 feet high, covers a third of an acre, and has a half mile of paths. And you are the pencil point—only you can't lift it off the page when you get stymied and fed up. You're trapped in there. The maze appealed to me when I first learned of it because it's like a kayak journey: You don't know how you're going to get from the beginning to the end, but you know there is a way and you assume you'll be clever enough to find it.

Actually, the maze was a lot harder than I thought it would be. Charts and formulae are available for help, but, as readers have perhaps noticed, I'm rather casual about making preparations beforehand when it comes to travel challenges. I just plunged in, assuming that my natural smarts would be sufficient to carry the day. Well, they almost weren't. In the middle, after some minutes of tramping around, I met a young German woman on holiday from Hamburg who was similarly lost, and we combined forces, assuming that two heads would be better than one. I'm afraid, however, that when it came to having knowledge to defeat the Hampton Court Maze, ours was a case of adding zero plus zero.

We kept walking and walking, taking one turn and then another, 'round and 'round. Eventually, through what should be called the trial-and-error method of solving the Hampton Court Maze, we did reach the exit.

Surrounding Hampton Court Palace are several square miles of parkland, and on the following morning, I returned to enjoy this green space. One of the first things I saw was deer in massive herds browsing on the grass and shrubs as calmly as cattle. One of the bucks had a huge rack—14 points as I later determined from inspecting the picture I took of him. I asked one of the guides outside the palace how they controlled the deer population.

"Oh, they're culled every year."

"How do you do that?"

"We shoot them."

This seemed a little crude. "You mean . . . with guns?"

He nodded.

"But don't people object? I mean, the animal lovers . . . ?"

He gave me a sly smile. "We don't tell people when we're doing it."

Another sight I came across on my walk that sunny Saturday morning was a throng of runners of all ages and sizes, including some moms pushing strollers, preparing for a 5K race. It was no ordinary one-time race, however, but a regular Saturday morning affair that had been going on for years. It was one of some hundred regular races taking place in parks all over England on Saturday mornings under the aegis of the voluntary group called Parkrun. The races incorporate a number of features that make them especially appealing to a wide range of participants. They are free, and no registration is necessary. You sign up once over the Internet and get a bar code ID, and then you can run on whatever Saturday you want. The digital tag enables the race organizers to enter everyone's times at the end of the race, which are posted on the Internet. The organizers give out various prizes to motivate the runners. One particularly coveted award is a T-shirt given to those who participate in 100 runs: That's about two years of Saturday morning runs.

The race organization has another unusual feature, as several runners proudly pointed out to me that morning: The runs are managed entirely by volunteers. This—and the fact that runners get to know one another over time—may explain the exuberant, convivial mood of the competitors as they gathered before the race.

The inventor of this brilliant system that makes running challenging and fun is Paul Sinton-Hewitt, a super-volunteer, one of Parkrun's major financial supporters, and also a serious runner himself. I was delighted to discover that the place where he started the nationwide program was right where I was standing, in Hampton's Bushy Park. That first race, in 2004, had 13 runners. At the run I observed on June 11, 2011, there were more than 800 participants—all happily oblivious to the memory of the tyrant who used to live in the palace across the park.

14
Olga

Anyone searching for the soul of England these days needs to explore rather cautiously, for the people you meet working in the shops and walking the streets are not necessarily English. This point was brought home to me emphatically on my visit to Windsor Castle.

Probably no building represents the spirit of the country more authentically than this castle, which William the Conqueror originally built in 1066, as a fortification to secure control of the River Thames. Since those times, the castle has been the headquarters of a succession of British monarchs, and is today the queen's preferred weekend residence.

When my paddling brought me to the town of Windsor, the castle was the first sight I planned to see. After spending the night at a B&B, I walked up to the main entrance the following morning and bought my admission ticket. Standing at the gate was a young female official, fitted in the traditional black gabardine uniform with red piping that the castle guides wear. To my mind, the young woman was the quintessential representative of the queen—standing for everything English. I happened to ask her a question and noticed a heavy accent when she replied.

"Where are you from?" I asked.

"Italy," she said.

"Well, uh . . ." I said. "*Buon giorno!*" We both laughed. She explained that she had been in England two years.

The widespread presence of immigrants is now a fact of English life. A country that was once highly homogeneous, socially and culturally, has in recent times accepted huge numbers of foreign-born, and this is changing its complexion. Among the first to come in large numbers were natives from the British West Indies in the 1950s. This surge was followed by an influx of Indian and Pakistani citizens in the 1960s and1970s. The English were just getting used to these dark-skinned peoples when, in the 1990s, another wave of immigrants began to arrive from all over Europe, especially from eastern European countries like Lithuania, Slovakia, and the Czech Republic. Following Poland's entry into the European Union in 2004, some half million Poles came to Britain.

Eavesdropping on an Internet chat room of young eastern Europeans, I caught this exchange between two young men:

> *Gaspoo*: Bournemouth is on my list of favorite cities
> . . . for many reasons . . . not just the international
> students . . .
> *Szwedw*: Did you say there are Swedish girls?
> *Gaspoo*: Of course, and Norwegian, and Polish, and
> Czech, and Chinese, and Thai and . . . it's the UK
> after all.

Thus did the correspondent note the reality that Britain is now a multiethnic society.

Tourists are likely to encounter immigrants because they have largely taken over the hospitality industry, especially in urban areas. My own trip traced this demographic. In the small towns and villages far from London, such as Cricklade and Newbridge, the pubs and lodgings were run, almost entirely, by native English. As the Thames carried me closer to London, the proportion of foreigners increased, especially in the larger towns. In Oxford, for example, it seemed that most of the people working in hotels, restaurants, and teashops were immigrants. In London, not just the shop employees are foreign-born, but most of the pedestrians as well.

I had many exchanges with immigrants, all pleasant and cordial, but also quite brief. In only one case did I have an extended contact. She was the ex-girlfriend of Alex, the man I met on the Wey Navigation canal. Perhaps I should say that Olga was Alex's should-have-been ex-girlfriend, because from the beginning I doubted her suitability as a mate. Meeting her was a strange experience, for Olga was a tense person to begin with, and I encountered her at a time of stress in her life. I found myself walking on eggshells when she was near.

On my first day in Hampton, Alex had been away in London when I let myself into his house, and I didn't see him until he returned home that evening. He was a lawyer who had just been discharged from a law firm, and had spent the day in the city to interview for another job. I asked him what had happened that caused him to lose his job.

"The executive of the firm wanted a yes-man, and I wasn't, really. That's what it was. We finally had this big blowup over a case where he wanted this thing and I told him it was the wrong way to go, and I wasn't going to change my view. So he gave me the boot."

When hearing a fired employee explain the reason for his dismissal, especially if he's someone you know little about, one wonders whether he's giving an accurate report. In Alex's case, I did have a piece of information that rather conclusively proved he was reporting correctly. It came from our meeting in the lock on the Wey Navigation, when I severely criticized his favorite book. Instead of diplomatically letting my remarks pass, Alex went out of his way to calmly but firmly contradict me. So the one thing I knew about him was that, indeed, he was not a yes-man.

The more I got to know Alex, the better I liked him. He had a generous nature—as reflected in his invitation to stay in his home. In our conversation that evening, another instance of his openhandedness emerged. On the way to the train station that morning, Alex had been accosted by a man who said he had a sick father in Manchester, and needed ten pounds for the rail fare. Alex bought the story and gave the man the money.

"But then," Alex continued, "I had second thoughts. Something about him didn't seem quite right. So I decided to follow him, and see where he went."

Alex shadowed him for a few minutes, and came to the conclusion that his petitioner was not behaving like someone urgently trying to get to Manchester to see a dying father. A policeman was sitting in a patrol car nearby, and Alex explained his concern to him. The policeman reported that the man was a well-known local scofflaw, and the two of them confronted the man about his confidence trick. They were sufficiently intimidating to persuade him to give back the ten pounds. "Of course, there were no grounds for prosecution," said Alex authoritatively, "but he didn't know that."

I took Alex to supper at a local restaurant (I could see from the bare refrigerator that Alex was not into cooking), where he explained a legal problem a friend had dumped in his lap. The friend was Olga, an immigrant from the Ukraine, whose daughter, Misha, had just been turned down in her application for law school at Oxford. Olga thought Oxford had acted wrongly in rejecting her daughter and wanted to challenge the decision.

"She really shouldn't be so concerned," said Alex. "Misha has already been accepted at LSE [London School of Economics], which is a perfectly fine, highly regarded law school. And Misha's content with going to LSE. But Olga has this thing about getting her daughter into Oxford. To her, it's the end-all and be-all."

We returned home, and I went to bed while Alex stayed up, poring over the documents pertaining to Misha's Oxford candidacy. I was impressed with Alex's willingness to help a friend in this way, but it seemed likely to be a futile exercise, given that university admissions are bound to be somewhat subjective and arbitrary.

The next morning was Saturday, and we were having coffee when Olga arrived. I was introduced and we shook hands. She was a short, trim woman in her 50s, with yellowish-blond hair in a permanent wave. I think she would have been pretty if she smiled, but I never saw her smile. Her English was fairly good, though she had a definite accent. We hardly spoke because she soon drew Alex into a conversation about her daughter's admissions case, right at the dining room table. She had brought another document pertaining to the case and handed it to him.

"They can't do a thing like that, Alex," she said, her voice rising.

"But Olga," said Alex, "You have to realize that the admissions committee has jurisdiction, so you can't. . . ."

She interrupted him, waving a paper. "Look, there is her score, 156.7. Now look over here"—she pulled out another paper—

"it gives the reserved alternative level of 151.0. That is totally inconsistent!"

Alex silently examined the paper. Olga was raising her voice. "There has to be a way to put a stop to this! If they have rules, they should follow them, shouldn't they, Alex? Shouldn't they?"

"Well, let me look this over," said Alex, calmly.

"We have to draft a letter," Olga said. "You know how to put these things, to make these people listen. They can't just go around doing things like this!" Alex didn't say anything.

After she left, Alex told me something of her background. She had come to England with her two children ten years ago to join her Ukrainian husband, who had found work in the construction industry. The marriage broke up after a few years—apparently it was rather stormy—and Olga raised the children, now grown.

Though Olga could be admired as a determined and protective single mother, I couldn't sympathize with her fixation about Oxford. She seemed highly subjective, viewing the world only in terms of her family goals and aspirations. Also, I found it hard to sympathize with her ambition of getting her child into a prestigious university because I'm rather skeptical of prestigious anything.

The conversation drifted to other things, and I found myself asking Alex if he had ever been married. He answered no.

"Have you wanted to?" I asked.

"Yes, I have. Very much, as a matter of fact. But somehow it never happened."

"Have you been serious about anyone?"

"Not really. It seems that the appropriate person never seems to turn up."

"Have you tried any, like, Internet dating?"

"I did that once, actually. It wasn't suitable at all."

I couldn't resist thinking that something was wrong with his search patterns. Here he was, an eligible bachelor, mid-40s, an economically secure, well-educated professional, and a pleasant, intelligent, generous person. He might not have had a movie-star appearance, being short, stocky, and somewhat balding, but that should be no barrier to finding a mate in the real world.

Alex laughed quietly to himself. "You know there was a time when I thought Olga might be someone who would work out.

"I'll tell you," he continued, "when Olga and I were getting somewhat serious, she was highly persistent in trying to dig out of me how much I was worth. Oh my, how she tried! But I was too clever for her. I didn't give anything away." I looked away so he wouldn't see me rolling my eyes. Now I *knew* there was something wrong with his search patterns.

During the morning meeting with Olga, Alex had mentioned that the community orchestra in nearby Teddington was giving a performance, and the three of us had arranged to attend it that evening. We drove to the church where the concert was to be held, a lovely old Church of England chapel, practically a cathedral, which had been decommissioned and was used for arts events. I offered to pay for everybody, but Olga insisted on paying for her ticket. Most of the seats had been taken, so we had to divide, with me sitting apart, and Olga and Alex sitting together. This made it seem they were a couple—an outcome that bothered me a little. It seemed to me that Alex with his sturdy English virtues needed to be protected from an unhealthy foreign tie.

After the concert—it was mostly Beethoven, including his Seventh Symphony—we shared our views of the performance. Alex and I found it creditable, but Olga was disappointed. "It wasn't, I don't know how to say it, inspiring. It was flat."

Driving home together, I expressed my interest in going the following morning to the Sunday sung Eucharist service in the Henry VIII chapel at Hampton Palace. "I go to that church," Olga said.

"Really?' I said, quite surprised. "What is your background? Are you Orthodox, or what?"

"I went to there in the Ukraine," she said, "but here it's no good. I don't like it. I go to Church of England."

She volunteered to pick me up for the service.

When she arrived at the house the following day, she went first to Alex, who was at the dining room table, finishing breakfast. I was on the couch in the living room with a newspaper.

There was a quiet exchange of words between them, and then suddenly Olga was shouting at him in highly emotional, angry tones.

"How can you say such a thing, Alex!? You are as bad as they are!"

Alex replied calmly, "But Olga, you have to see their point of view. . . ."

Olga interrupted, shouting louder. "It's absolutely disgraceful what you are saying! Alex, you are terrible. Terrible! And you say you are my friend! How can you say you are my friend!?" She glanced at me through the open door to the living room. I didn't want to be listening to this, but there was no polite way to escape. I ducked my head deeper behind the *Telegraph.*

Alex quietly responded. "But Olga, there's only one committee that retains jurisdiction, and . . ."

"Alex, how can you?! You are a very cruel man, Alex. That is all I'm going to say. Very, very cruel!" Then she moved into the hall and glanced over at me, "Are you coming?"

I followed her to the door and out to her car. She said nothing, and I was careful not to utter a word. In her explosive mood, I felt she was capable of taking a bite out of my arm. After all, Alex, her generous friend, had gone well beyond the call of duty to help her with such a hopeless cause, only to earn a diatribe. What would happen to me, a mere acquaintance, if I roused her ire?

As we drove over to Hampton Court in perfect, stony silence, it occurred to me that Alex was giving yet more evidence that he was not a yes-man. Any person with less integrity—me, for example—would have simply agreed with her to evade her tirade.

The dying religion that is the Church of England produces a number of anomalies. One of them occurs whenever a church is part of a famous tourist attraction. You have millions of people who want to gawk at the attraction and are willing to pay many pounds to do so, and a tiny handful who want to worship at the church who can't be asked to pay anything. The management of these establishments finesses this dilemma by having a special line for those who present themselves as worshippers at service times. Thus, if you're willing to appear to be an observant Christian, you get into this expensive tourist site free. If you actually are one, so much the better.

I made use of this system three times on my trip: once to attend an evensong at St. George's Chapel at Windsor Castle, once to attend evensong at Westminster Abbey, and on this morning to attend the sung Eucharist at Henry VIII Chapel in Hampton Court Palace.

Olga knew all about this arrangement, and with her expression grim she led me silently from the parking lot through various courtyards to the portal with the special guard who admitted worshippers only. At the other end of the building was the long line of tourists waiting to pay £16 to get in.

"We go this way," said Olga, still without any trace of warmth in her voice. I obediently followed her, and we were soon at the magnificent chapel, which was closed to tourists for the duration of the service. There were about 40 worshippers, most of whom were first-time visitors, but the numbers also included a dozen regulars, mostly elderly ladies. The rector was warmly greeting them exactly as he would at a village church in the countryside, nicely oblivious to the fact that we stood at ground zero of a mega-tourist site in the chapel of a notorious despot.

Olga headed for a front-row seat at the side of the choir, and I followed her. My interest in attending the service was to hear the traditional choral chants, Psalms, and anthems. In the more prominent Church of England houses of worship, this music is performed at the highest level. The singers of the lower parts are paid male professionals; the soprano part is sung by boys from an affiliated private school. These little boys are instructed in singing for many hours each day, so they too might as well be accounted as professionals. I had been so impressed with this music—you just cannot match the angelic purity of the boy soprano voice—that I had recorded these performances at other services with my digital recorder, solely to enjoy them again later.

This practice had caused no problem in the other churches. Hardly anyone noticed the little device I set beside me on the pew, and in the laid-back context of the modern Church of England, I was sure no one minded. But now I was seated next to Olga, and something told me she was likely to be more popish than the pope when it came to observing decorum in her adopted English church. And she was in a foul mood besides. I feared that if she saw me operating the recorder she would scold me for violating the sanctity of the Henry VIII Chapel.

By moving carefully and surreptitiously, I was able to record the singing without catching her notice. Just before each song was to begin, I would turn the device on with it still in my pocket, slowly slide it out onto the pew, and then block her view of it with the service program held in my left hand. Perhaps I shouldn't give myself too much credit for evading her notice because she was very self-absorbed and paid little attention to me throughout the service. When I lacked the necessary songbook to sing a hymn, it was the woman in the pew behind who handed me the a book opened to the right page. Olga was not even aware I had a problem.

After the service was over, Olga's mood seemed to have improved slightly, and I ventured to ask her the favor of dropping me off in Kingston, a nearby town that I wanted to visit. This she agreed to do. On the drive over, we made small talk, though I was careful not to mention anything about Oxford, her daughter, her ex-husband, her job, how she liked England, Alex, her past, or her future. I think we talked about the weather. She dropped me off on a main street in Kingston, said goodbye, and that was the last I saw of Olga. I walked away, relieved to be alone but also feeling a little guilty that I couldn't like her. The best I could do, adopting a benevolent perspective, was to feel sorry for her, as such a prisoner of narrow needs that she wasn't able to relax and enjoy life's offerings.

After spending the afternoon enjoying the sights in Kingston, I walked back to Alex's house in Hampton. When I entered, I found him working in his study. I immediately brought up Olga's outburst earlier that morning.

"Wasn't that awful?" I said. "I couldn't believe it! How could anyone behave like that?"

Alex gave a relaxed chuckle. "Yes, she was way over the line. And she knew it. She came back later and apologized."

"Oh, she did?" I was eager to get a concrete picture of this apology, to be able to gauge its depth and sincerity, but Alex had no interest in elaborating. Instead, he turned to the papers on his desk.

"You know, I've been studying her case some more, and Olga *does* have a point."

I was stunned. It made no sense that he should continue to labor on her behalf after her scolding.

"Alex," I said sternly. "What *are* you doing!?"

He ignored my reproach and pointed to the paper. "Really, look at this. From a certain point of view, a case can be made. If you consider the averages of the admitted candidates, and then compare Misha's score on the alternative examination . . ."

I refused to be drawn in. I marveled at Alex's patience, persistence, and generosity, but I wasn't going to expend my brainpower trying to master this hopeless cause being pressed for highly subjective motives. I excused myself and retreated to the living room to finish reading the *Telegraph*.

I have just two further items of information to impart about the Alex-Olga relationship, which Alex passed along to me months later. First, after a very burdensome effort, the appeal to have Misha admitted to Oxford was rejected, and she happily accepted the admission at the London School of Economics.

Second, two months after calmly suffering Olga's explosive harangue, Alex went on an extended holiday trip to the Ukraine with her.

15
Grappling with the Tidal Thames

The following morning, Alex had to leave the house at an early hour to pursue his job hunting in London. We said goodbye and I stayed behind to load the dishwasher, and then to peruse daytime TV as inane as that of my homeland. There was no point in an early departure—my route was blocked by the tidal weir at Richmond, just a few miles downriver. Until the tide came up in the early afternoon, the weir would be closed to boat traffic. After 10 a.m., I let myself out of the house and walked to the rowing club where my kayak had safely passed the weekend. In a few minutes, I was waterborne again, ready to tackle the tidal section of the river through London.

I'd been apprehensive about this stretch of the river since the beginning of my trip. Until now, I had been paddling on flat water, where each segment of the river was quietly backed up behind a weir. Below Richmond, where greater London begins, the Thames is a natural estuary, open to the sea and its incoming and outrushing tides. These tides are amplified by the narrowing effect of the funnel-like estuary, so they reach great heights—a surge of 6 meters at London Bridge. This meant that the piers and banks where I might be able to land at high tide would be 19 feet above my head at low tide. I also feared that the river bottom at low tide would be covered by a layer of deep, sticky mud, which I might not be able to walk across. If I didn't get off the river before low tide, I could be trapped at the bottom of that muddy canyon for six hours, and then face the inrushing tidal current pushing me back up the river.

A second anxiety involved turbulence. The night before, I had discussed the following day's travel with Alex. At one point he pushed his glasses up over his forehead, and looked carefully at me: "I don't want to say this, Jim, but you should know there are some very nasty currents by Blackfriars Bridge."

Because he was a sportsman and a rower, his warning had a ring of authority. I knew his general point was valid. Upriver of Richmond, the Thames is a placid recreational body of water, a no-wake zone, with all powerboats restricted to less than 5 mph. Closer to London, no speed limits apply, and the big powerboats and tour boats can set up some pretty big waves. I was definitely planning to wear my life jacket when on this stretch.

Stopping in London, I would not only have to find a way to climb out of the river channel, but also find a safe place to leave my kayak. Up river, I could usually find a clump of willows to slip the boat behind, or an out-of-the-way pasture where few if anyone would see it overnight. In London proper, all I could visualize was bare concrete prowled by shiftless villains inclined to steal anything on general principle.

Another worry was—forgive my directness, but—how was I supposed to go to the bathroom? The river is a naked, stone-sided channel that passes through a city of 8 million people, whose numbers are swelled by hundreds of thousands of tourists. These tourists, armed with cameras, throng the sidewalks and bridges overlooking the Thames, and are eager to take pictures of anything interesting or amusing. Talk about a YouTube opportunity! The need for restroom facilities is a problem never mentioned in historical accounts of famous explorations across seas and journeys to poles. Such accounts are meticulous in detailing many features of the expeditions, reporting how many dozen cutlasses were stowed aboard, and how many hogsheads of wine. But the chronicles are silent about bodily functions. Nobody asks, "Where did Cortéz go to the bathroom?" Maybe it's not a life-threatening issue, but in this day of civilized standards, it must be dealt with, and the problem weighed on me as I approached the outskirts of London.

On the way to Richmond, I had two chance encounters that added intelligence about the waters by London—one encouraging, the other unsettling. Brian, the driver of an empty tour boat going through the Teddington Lock with me—my 44th and last lock—reported that the bed of the river alongside London is shingle—that is, pebbles. On reflection, it made sense that the scouring of the rapid tidal current would drag most of the mud farther out the estuary. So at least I would be able to walk around at low tide, even if I was trapped down in a canyon.

Some minutes after putting Teddington Lock behind me, I met up with a ferryboat for pedestrians—just an ordinary runabout with an outboard motor—and struck up a conversation with the driver and his two passengers. The driver told me to watch out for the chop on the water down in central London.

"How high is it?" I asked. "Like this?" I held my hand a foot over the water next to my kayak.

He emphatically shook his head. He stretched out his hand and held it four feet above the surface. I frowned in disbelief, but he refused to lower the position of his hand.

As I approached the weir at Richmond, the first thing I saw was a bright orange line across the surface of the water in front of me. This line was painted along the top inches of the steel plates that were damming up the river. If these plates were not there, the water in the river above would drain away with the tide, leaving boats stranded at the bottom of a muddy channel. When the incoming tide reaches the same level as the water above the weir, the operator raises the plates into the structure above, and the river is unobstructed.

I paddled over to investigate a lock on the right side. I was hoping to find someone who could give me information about what to expect downriver, especially what I might do with the kayak overnight.

Next to the lock was an electric sign with bright red letters that read:

WEIRS CLOSED
USE LOCK
£5 CHARGE

I understood the logic of the sign: If you didn't want to wait until the tide came up for the plates to be lifted, you could go around them using the lock—for a charge. What I didn't grasp until later was what this sign implied about sociability and help-fulness of the employees.

I moored the kayak at the base of the lock and climbed an iron stairway to the top, expecting to find a cheerful, friendly lock-keeper. Instead, I encountered a sourpuss wearing the uniform of the Environment Agency.

"What are you doing here?" the man asked in a hostile tone. "You're not supposed to be here. This is a restricted area."

"I just wanted to ask when the weir is supposed to open." I said.

"It should have been opened already," the man said grouchily. I couldn't tell whether he was complaining about the weir operator for being slow at his job or criticizing the tide for being late. "But you can't be here," he continued. "How did you get in here, anyway? This is government property, closed to the public." His tone implied I was guilty of breaking and entering.

I pointed to my kayak nestled at the base of the lock, but this didn't mollify him. "You have to leave here. You can't be here. Boats wait on the other side." He pointed to a dock across the river.

As I paddled across to the other side, I reflected that I should have predicted this officiousness. Because boaters were being charged for using this lock, it followed that they wouldn't be allowed to run it themselves—as they could and did do on all the other locks. This left boaters in an inferior, dependent position, and put the lockkeeper in a position of authority. So the spirit of equality and friendship I had experienced at the earlier locks disappeared.

No one else was waiting for the weir to open, and no one else went through with me when the big steel plates finally rose into the gantry high above the water. This pointed up the fact that the Thames has two rather separate segments, with very little traffic between them. Upriver from Richmond is the nontidal Thames where rented narrowboats and rowing shells and skiffs ply the flat, tame water that lies between the weirs and locks. Downriver from Richmond, the Thames belongs to boats willing to grapple with tidal currents and the steep daily rise and fall of the water, that is, large tour boats, ocean-going cabin cruisers, and barges.

Shortly after leaving the Richmond weir, I paddled alongside the world-famous Kew Royal Botanic Gardens. I only saw trees and a jogging path alongside the river; the hothouses and formal gardens were some distance away. I went ashore since it was my last chance to use a forest before entering built-up London.

Back on the river, the outgoing tidal current began to help me, bringing my speed to 5.2 mph according to the GPS; by late afternoon, I had made it to the Chelsea area, where I planned to stop for the night. I had the idea of pulling off the river into what the map showed as an inlet and marina—Chelsea Creek, the map called it. But when I got there, I found that the inlet was blocked by the closed gates of a 20-foot-high lock. I should have guessed they would have this lock to maintain the water level inside the docking area. The only time they would open it would be at high tide, when the water level inside and outside was the same.

With that option nixed, I turned my attention to the floating docks that ran along the middle of the river. I could easily get off at any of these docks, but I would need to go through a security gate to make my way to the street. To do this, I would have to get the code from someone. At first, this seemed a promising possibility. All I would have to do is strike up a conversation with a friendly boat owner. But I found, much to my surprise, that all the boats were deserted. I paddled alongside scores of these boats, hoping to see someone coiling a rope or peering out a porthole, but not one human being could I find.

I drew the kayak up on some exposed shingle—it was getting near low tide by now—and walked over the muddy rocks to ask for advice from a man who was leaning over the rail above me. I figured I could just barely get the kayak over the sea wall at that spot, with help, to leave it for the night. But the man advised against it, pointing to the council estates lying just off the river—notorious as centers of crime and delinquency.

So I dragged the boat back into the water and continued farther down the river, hemmed in on both sides by 20-foot stone
walls. I was starting to feel pretty desperate when, just below the
Prince Albert Bridge, I spotted a steel stairway going up the face of
the wall to the street.

The outgoing tide was still sucking through the lowest steps
of this stairway. It was a terrible place to moor, but it was the only
solid mooring of any kind, and offered a way to the street. I kept
muttering to myself, "This is insane," as I went through the activi-
ties of unloading my day pack from the kayak and tying the boat
for the night. The tide on the river at this point had a rise of nearly
20 feet, so I was forced to tie my two short mooring lines together
to make a single one long enough to accommodate the range. (If I
tied the boat to a line down at the bottom of the stairway, it would
either tear the line or sink the boat when the tide rose.)

Whenever there is a real chance of losing the kayak by a mooring
line failure, I always use the two lines attached to two separate anchor
points. I felt reckless abandoning the boat to the River Thames and
the North Sea tied overnight on a single, slender line about 1/8-inch
thick. I tied this to the stairway 20 feet above the boat, about where
I figured the water level would reach at high tide. Theft of the boat
in this urban area was one problem; vandals untying it and letting
it drift away was another. But the biggest danger I saw was damage
or destruction to the boat as it went through the tide change, for it
could get hung up or wedged and then crushed by the rising water. I
especially feared that the boat would be swirled under the steel stairway, and then, when the tide tried to lift it, it would be crushed up
against the underside of the stairs. I turned to climb the stairs, giving one last look at the poor little kayak dangling by a single thread
at the bottom of the abyss. "This is insane," I repeated.

After climbing the stairs to the street level, I found a locked gate. I later discovered that this was the rule all along the urban Thames. There must be several dozen stairways on the lower Thames, some built at great expense, and every one has a locked gate at the top—so the stairway is, for most purposes, useless. Who has the key? I'm sure no one knows. So if Kate Middleton herself were to fall off the royal barge, swim to one of these stairways, and climb to the top, she would stand there shivering in her finery 'till the cows come home as officialdom struggled to contact the bureaucrat who might know which drawer in which back office held the key. In practice, of course, Kate in her designer dress and high heels would simply have to scramble over the parapet, which is what I did, aided by a strong-armed German tourist passing by on the street who answered my call for help.

I was in Belgravia, an upscale part of London. Following the directions of locals, I made my way along Chelsea Hospital Road and Pimlico Road to Ebury Street, where I noticed a plaque on a house stating that Wolfgang Amadeus Mozart composed his first symphony there in 1754. He was eight at the time. The first hotel I came upon seemed rather opulent, with a Georgian façade that made it look like a private mansion. I knew I was over my head as soon as I saw the receptionist, a drop-dead gorgeous model, dressed to the nines and meticulously coiffed. She was not standing behind a Formica-topped counter as in an ordinary hotel, but seated at her own spacious mahogany desk. I went through the motion of asking her how much a room would cost.

Her detachment was commendably neutral. Any ordinary hotel employee might have registered a flicker of disparagement at my disheveled, homeless look, and my luggage consisting of a rumpled backpack, but she was perfectly polite in her manner toward me.

"Four hundred ninety-five pounds," she said in a soft, rounded voice. That was around $800.

I gulped at this number, which was astronomically out of my price range, but taking my cue from her, I maintained a calm and dignified manner. "I think I'd better look elsewhere," I said with a smile.

As I walked away, I found myself puzzling over the room rate, trying to imagine what extra luxuries or services would justify that fantastic price. Perhaps they provided guests with a facecloth.

I walked along a few more blocks and, close to Victoria Station, found a typical low-budget hotel—one you can tell is a dump the minute you walk in—a former mansion divided and subdivided into a rabbit warren of cubicles, with floorboards creaking beneath the dingy carpet. The charge of £75 a night fit my pocketbook nicely. My room was on the third floor, and the bathroom I was supposed to use was down three flights on the second-floor landing. But when I got there, an "Out of Order" sign was propped over the toilet, which meant the facility for my use—for everybody's use—was two more flights down. It was one of those charming lodging disasters that years of commando camping experiences had taught me to accept with equanimity.

I eventually bedded down, my brain troubled with the vision of my tiny, helpless kayak tethered at the end of its 20-foot thread, swinging and swirling in the inrushing tide. Anxiety about the kayak was soon overpowered by exhaustion, however, and I fell into a stone-like sleep.

16

Sightseeing from One Inch above the Water

The following morning, before anyone in the hotel was up, I threw on my clothes and retraced my route of the previous day—past the house where Mozart lived, past the Chelsea Royal Hospital—to the stairway on the river. I was so sure I would not find a kayak, or at least not a useable one, that I didn't even have the courage to hum my optimistic little line about the flag still being there. As I neared the river, I could see it was low tide again, the shingle bottom of the river exposed. I peered over the parapet and saw something quite unexpected. The kayak was there—amazingly—but it was not resting on the mud-covered pebbles at the bottom. Instead, it was lying at the top of the stairs! Apparently, the incoming tide had swirled it over the stairway, and when the water retreated, it came to rest on the stairway, nose up. As far as I could tell, it was undamaged. I leapt over the stone parapet—I was getting pretty adept at this by now—inched the boat down the steps, and heaved it onto the shingle alongside the stairway, so it would float with the incoming tide. I was careful to tie the mooring line well up the stairway.

An hour later, after breakfast and checking out of the hotel, I was back to watch over the kayak as the incoming tide floated it. I read a bit, and visited with a road repair crew that was filling a pothole in the street next to me. At about 11, I suddenly realized that if I waited for the top of the tide I wouldn't be able to board the kayak because some pilings would be in the way. It was time to climb over the parapet and depart. I asked an older man coming down the sidewalk for help. He put up his hands, shaking his head. "No espik eenglis," he said. I recognized it as a Spanish accent and switched to that. Amazingly, he was from Peru, where I had spent a year during my college days. He was retired—a working-class fellow—and living with his daughter in London. After visiting with him a bit, I climbed over the parapet, and he handed my backpack over to me.

Loaded and launched, I found the incoming tidal current still too strong to oppose, so I paddled across to a floating dock and tied up to wait it out, seated in the boat, snacking and reading to pass the time. After several more hours, the tide turned, and I was off. It was a glorious afternoon with a clear sky and a nice sun . . . perfect tourist weather.

Ahead of me, I first saw the towers of Westminster Abbey, then the gingerbread Victorian architecture of the Houses of Parliament, and Big Ben, which showed the time as 2:15. Just as I passed, the clock struck the quarter hour, and boy, was I disappointed. The chime cadence has been copied in towers on town squares and college campuses all over the world, and in millions of home clocks. Almost all these chimes have clear, musical tones, so I expected a beautiful, memorable sound from this famous grandfather of all these timepieces. But it was not so. Big Ben's notes sounded dull and raspy, like somebody hitting an oil pipeline with a sledgehammer.

I scooted under Westminster Bridge, which had bright red double-decker buses crawling along the top of it. I emerged from under the bridge to see the London Eye, the 443-foot-high Ferris wheel. It is reportedly the most popular tourist attraction in London, and its prices reflect it. A 30-minute ride in one of its capsules to reach the highest observation point in London costs £28.50 per person or £114 for a family of four. As I slipped below the Eye, it occurred to me that I was breaking a record in the other direction: At one inch above the water, my kayak was undoubtedly the lowest observation point in London.

To my left, I saw the Egyptian obelisk known as Cleopatra's Needle, and, behind that, the spire of St. Martin in the Fields, the famous church on Trafalgar Square. Next, I saw the giant dome of St. Paul's Cathedral, and, behind it, the bullet-shaped skyscraper known as the Gherkin (because it resembles a cucumber). I couldn't spend too much time gaping at the sights, however, because the river was crowded with boats, mostly long tour boats, sometimes coming two or even three abreast, as well as with barges and stationary obstructions tied up to buoys in the river. I had to plan my route way ahead to avoid them all. I saw no other kayaks or any other small boats on the water. I was all alone with the big boys, like an ant running around under elephants' legs. The outgoing tidal current had picked up speed, so I would have no chance of stopping or turning around. I was zipping under the bridges, one after the other, each bridge thronged with tourists taking pictures of me to show folks back home.

At Blackfriars Bridge, the chop became quite serious, even though there was no wind. The waves were caused by the many tour boats whose combined wakes echo and re-echo with undiminished strength off the stone walls on both sides. But there were no breaking waves, so my boat rode happily and dry on top of the turbulence.

The glorious tourist miles soon came to an end as I slid past the HMS *Belfast*, a battleship permanently moored across the river from the Tower of London, and passed under the ornate Tower Bridge, waving back at the tourists waving at me. I had always assumed that this medieval-looking bridge dated back to ancient times. But in visiting it a few days later, I discovered that it was constructed in 1894, deliberately designed to look like it came out of a fairy tale. This imitation angered professional architects of the day—one said, "It represents the vice of tawdriness and pretentiousness"—but the whole world loves it now.

Tower Bridge is the last bridge across the River Thames as it widens out into a broad estuary. Now I was in the Docklands, the area of London where ships used to dock and unload. They did not dock on the river, but at high tide entered huge lagoons—some more than a mile long and hundreds of yards wide—which were then closed by lock gates so the unloading ships would not be affected by the fall of the tide on the river. Then, at later high tides, the gates would open and ships would steam out. After 1980, all the ship traffic moved far down the estuary to Tilbury and to other ports around the coast, so the Docklands became derelict land. It is now being gradually urbanized—mainly, as far as I could see, with four-story apartment buildings. This area also contains the Millenium Dome, an entertainment venue that I paddled alongside for what seemed like miles.

Farther downriver, on my left, I saw the baroque domes and stately white quadrangle of the Old Royal Naval College at Greenwich. Behind these buildings, up on the hill, stands the famous Royal Observatory, which defined Greenwich mean time and also the prime meridian. To check on the astronomers, I slipped my GPS out of its case and watched the changing readout of my longitude as I paddled along. First it said W (west) 000 degrees, 00 minutes, and 03 seconds; a few moments later, it read 02 seconds, then 01, and then the dial read 000 00 00 as I crossed the line that separates the western hemisphere from the eastern.

The only other point of interest, and the goal of my trip, was the Thames Barrier, two miles farther down the river. The Thames Barrier is a system of gates that can be closed for a few hours during unusual conditions of high tide to keep the sea back and reduce flooding in London. It is activated about four times a year. I had read about this facility and learned that it was operated by the government's Environment Agency and had more than 60 employees, which seemed rather a lot, considering that their only job is to push a button once every few months.

Gliding through the open gates of the Barrier took but a moment, but then my problems began. I needed to find a landing place. It was after 6 p.m., and I had been sitting on my behind in the boat for eight hours. All I could see, all the way down the river on both sides, were 20-foot-high stone walls. As far as I knew, they went on forever. I concluded that I would be better off going back through the Barrier to a place about a half mile upriver where I had noticed a possible landing spot. However, when I turned around and tried to paddle upstream, I could barely make any headway in the still-strong tidal current. So I pulled aside to the slack water at the edge of the Barrier to rest. My idea was to wait out the tide for another half hour or so, and then try to go back upstream. I saw a man standing on a walkway above me.

"Could you give me some advice?" I asked. "Do you know if there's a place I can take my boat out of the river?"

"You can't come out here," he said sternly. "You can't touch any part of this property." (Apparently, canvas American kayaks contaminate barriers.) "We're going to watch you all the time on CCTV," he said, and then he turned on his heel and walked into the building.

I frowned, rather amazed at this hostile, unhelpful response. Because the man had not specifically ordered me to leave, I figured I could remain where I was, floating in the slack water, but I didn't feel very comfortable about it. I could see them—all 60 employees—leaving their smoke break at the vending machines and gathering around the closed circuit TV screen to watch me. They finally had an important job to do . . . monitor a kayak in nearby waters.

Modern bureaucracy is fixated with terrorism, no matter how illogical the anxiety. In the case of the Thames Barrier, the agency folk hadn't figured out that it was about the least significant terrorist target in the country. Disabling it by an explosion would, at best, result in a few wet basements in London some months later. Any bus, or even a taxicab, would be a more attention-getting target.

But Thames Barrier employees felt that allowing a kayaker to rest a few moments beside their facility represented too great a threat. Communications were undoubtedly flashing up and down the chain of command of the Environment Agency—perhaps even to the minister of defense. A police boat pulled away from a dock below the Barrier and came toward me, strobe light flashing. I politely paddled over to him because he couldn't enter the shallows where I was resting.

I explained to the captain standing on the bridge that I was making a trip down the Thames—a declaration that had elicited sentiments of admiration and helpfulness from everyone else along the river. Here it earned me no sympathy.

"You're being a nuisance," the captain shouted out to me. "You shouldn't be here!"

"I'm just trying to find a way to get my kayak off the river. Do you know where I could do that?"

"You should have made preparations beforehand. You should have contacted the authorities to arrange something, to get permission." (I could just see myself writing a letter: "Dear Environment Agency, United Kingdom.")

"Well, what should I do?" This expression of helplessness didn't melt his heart of stone.

"You can't stay here," he replied. "You're a nuisance. We have the security of the Barrier to tend to. You can't stay here."

I didn't know what my rights were—I assumed I was free to occupy any part of the river, and there weren't any signs saying I couldn't be in these waters. If I didn't move, what were they going to do? Shoot me?

It occurred to me that I could claim to be in personal danger, fearing for my safety—which was slightly true, of course—and thus compel the welfare state to take care of me. But I had no desire to place myself in these bureaucrats' hands. To perish adrift in the North Sea seemed a much healthier alternative. I gave a sigh and paddled away down the river.

After a half mile, I spotted a stairway leading up the stone wall—two facing stone stairways, actually—that descended and met at the bottom. I thought I could, with help, carry the kayak up those stairs. I asked a man seated on a bench above me if the gate was open. He examined it and shouted back that it was locked with a chain. He helpfully went around to the gate on the other stairway and found it also was securely locked.

A half mile farther, I came upon a long concrete boat launch ramp on the north side of the river. Amazingly, this ramp extended up to the street level and was unblocked by any gate or chain. This proved to be my point of deliverance from the Thames, the perfect takeout spot for my needs.

Just as I finished taking apart the boat and fitting the pieces into the carrying pack, a young couple came down the ramp to see what I was doing. They were just starting a life together in East London. Emily was working in the schools as a freelance dance instructor, organizing introductory dance sessions for children. Theo worked as a video game programmer. They told me there was a Docklands Light Railway station a mile away, and I resolved to use it to get back to my reserved hotel room in London.

Emily and Theo accompanied me all the way to the station, to be sure I didn't lose my way, showing me which bridges to cross over the huge rectangular lakes that used to be the docks. The pack got extremely heavy, cutting into my shoulders, and I had to sit down on the pavement to rest several times. I'm sure Theo—a strapping young lad—would have been glad to carry my pack if I had asked him, but I was too proud to ask for help—and he was too polite to intrude by offering to carry my personal property.

At the Gallions Reach Station, the youngsters showed me the lift (it was an elevated train in this suburb of London), and we said goodbye. Then began an unbelievably grueling two-hour struggle to lug the kayak pack as well as my backpack and fanny pack through the London Underground system. I had to take four different trains, walk up stairs and down stairs, and through long passageways, with the straps of the kayak always burning into my shoulders. At the stations, I had to wait for the train with the pack strapped to my back, since there was no other way to carry it onto the train. In the central part of the city, the subway cars were still crowded even though it was well past rush hour, and I couldn't get a seat. After pushing my way into the crowded car, I would remove the pack in the only possible way, by sitting on the floor and wriggling out of the straps. When it was time to get off the car, I had to reverse the process, starting by sitting on the floor. The other passengers must have been mystified by the humongous, scruffy black pack, wondering what it might contain. I imagined them assuming I was an itinerant homeless person laid low by drug and alcohol abuse, pathologically restless and unable to settle down, who had crammed all his worthless worldly possessions into this pack. It was very embarrassing.

At 9:30 p.m., with the pack on my back, dizzy with fatigue, I staggered into my little hotel by Victoria Station, somewhat amazed that I had maintained the stamina to accomplish such a grueling portage on top of a full day of kayaking and arguing with the Environment Agency. By rights, it seemed that I should have been lying unconscious somewhere in the Underground, stricken by a medical condition ending in –ia. I credited my survival to the mavens of physical fitness who had kept me in shape all year long back home—the leaders of exercise classes, yoga instructors, and Judy, my wife and ever-vigilant nutritionist.

Several days later, my mind went back to the uncomfortable scene at the Thames Barrier, and it dawned on me how strikingly unusual it was. In my 29 days of travel, I needed help scores and

scores of times, and every time courteous English people—and foreigners, too—stepped forward to assist me. Against this consistent
outpouring of aid, this one rude, deliberately unhelpful response
was a strange contrast indeed.

What makes it doubly puzzling is that, in being rude and unco-
operative, *the workers were acting against their own goals.* Consider
this: The excellent slipway where I landed the kayak lay just a mile
below the Barrier. Surely the Environment Agency employees,
experts on the river, knew about this obvious structure right in
their backyard.

So they were in possession of the information needed to solve
both their problem and mine, but they failed to make use of it.
When I asked the first employee for help, he could have informed
me of this takeout spot, and thus earned my gratitude, as well as
clearing my troublesome image from the CCTV cameras. And
when the security officers came in the police boat to chase me
away, they also could have gotten me out of their hair in a polite
and helpful way by directing me to this landing place. So why
didn't they?

I think the answer is that they didn't see me as a human being.
They didn't see me as someone to take an interest in, as someone
with a problem they could help solve. They were blind creatures
of bureaucracy, and I was simply a foreign object, like a bother-
some stump that might have drifted down the river and jammed
their gates.

If the workers I met had a helpful attitude toward outsid-
ers like me, they could have come away from the contact with
a socially rewarding experience. They would have been able to
go home to their families and proudly report, "We helped a kayaker from America today, a fellow that's gone all the way down

the Thames from the beginning!" Instead, locked in their self-important, impersonal mind-set, they came away with a negative impression. They had another dull day at work, made a little more frustrating, as they would scornfully recount, by "a dumb American in a kayak."

It might not be easy to transform an agency like the Thames Barrier to encourage the workers to treat people as people. But it seems that in this age of bureaucracy, we ought to be thinking about such strategies. Part of the answer might be to take inspiration from the locks along the Thames and involve volunteers and bystanders in the operation. In this way, employees might learn to relate to visitors as equals, and even friends.

More broadly, following in the footsteps of Thameside philosophers like William Morris and Tom Rolt, we need to be thinking how we can put human relationships first in our world. Bureaucracy is a threat to genuine interactions, but it's not the only one. Another challenge comes from the electronic devices that have engulfed us, devices that give the appearance of enhancing communication while they in fact stifle and trivialize it. Then there is urbanization with its curious power to dehumanize. It's a paradox, really, how cities, by pushing people ever closer together, can render them more distant.

In this effort to resist the lure of convenience and modernity, I think it likely that we shall find the English playing a leading role. As we have discovered, they tend to have traits that suit them for this task: a social confidence that makes them unafraid to appear eccentric, and an affection for tradition that supports a healthy skepticism of the modern. These qualities have already produced many English rebels willing to question the blind thrust of technology. Morris and Rolt were two such leaders, but there have been many others. For example, the two great 20th-century novels warning against the abuses of science and bureaucracy were penned by Englishmen.

In 1949, George Orwell wrote *1984*, a novel dramatizing the dehumanizing danger of centralized state control. A decade earlier, in 1936, Aldous Huxley published *Brave New World*. In Huxley's regimented future civilization, originality and creativity are suppressed. Nobody falls in love any more, books have disappeared, Shakespeare is forgotten, and writing poetry is a crime. The populace is entertained by an electronic audiovisual simulator of sexual pleasure called the "feelies."

Though read by scores of millions, Orwell and Huxley's calls for a return to humane values and human-scale institutions have perhaps not been well heeded as yet. But the soil from whence they sprang contains many more such seeds of independence.

Mark my words. One of these days you are going to open your newspaper (all right, scroll down) and read about an unusual movement cropping up in England where people have deliberately adopted an awkward, old-fashioned, non–electronic approach to life's challenges, and are having the time of their lives.